CW00591977

COLOUR
YOUR
WORLD

A

COLOR YOUR WORLD

Frank Don

Destiny Books
New York

Destiny Books
377 Park Avenue South
New York, NY 10016

First quality paperback edition: October 1983

Copyright © 1977 by Frank Don

All rights reserved. No part of this book may be reproduced or utilized in
any form or by any means, electronic or mechanical, including photo-
copying and recording or by any information storage and retrieval system, without permission in writing from the publisher. Inquiries should
be addressed to Destiny Books.

10 9 8 7 6 5 4 3 2 1

Library of Congress Cataloging in Publication Data

Don, Frank.
  Color your world.
  Bibliography: p.
  1. Color—Psychological aspects.   I. Title.
BF789.C7D58   1983   152.1'45   83-18942
ISBN 0-89281-048-3

Destiny Books is a division of Inner Traditions International, Ltd.

Printed and bound in the United States of America.

This book is dedicated to the reader. With an increased understanding of color may you paint your life with greater beauty and enjoyment.

Contents

COLOR
YOUR
WORLD

Chapter 1

The World In Color

Each day we awaken to a vibrant, pulsating world of sights, sounds, and sensations of all description. Although our world is continually changing, an integral part of this changing world is color. Ranging a spectrum of infra-red to ultra-violet, color can make all things bright and beautiful and affects all creatures great and small. Since life daily paints a multicolored mural of nature, we find ourselves in the midst of a master artist's rendering. Like the mixtures of the artist's palette, our lives are colored by gradations and shadings. Our emotional state and psychological well-being range a spectrum of ecstasy to despair. Yet by increased awareness we can gain greater control over our feelings and our state of being. As our perceptions become amplified by the myriad of colors surrounding us, so too can we become masters of our lives by recognizing the effects and uses of color upon us.

Everything in nature partakes of color. In the plant kingdom this fact is obvious. Trees, bushes, flowers are all considered in terms of their color. Consider, if you will, the impressions in your mind when you think of different trees, plants, or flowers. If you were asked to describe your mental images, wouldn't you at some point in your enumeration of characteristics include color? You probably would, for the colors of the plant world hold a great appeal for all of us. We buy flowers in order to "add a bit of color" to our homes. To provide new colors in flowers, horticulturists constantly seek new strains of a genus of flower. The artistic landscaping and blend of colors have made cultivated gardens popular tourist attractions.

In the fall in the northeastern United States people stream out of the cities to view the changing of the seasons in the countryside. For the lush green of a New England summer turns to an autumnal spectacle of yellows, oranges, and reds. In the springtime in the South one thinks of the colorful blossoming of the magnolias and azaleas. And in the Rocky Mountains who could forget the contrast in late summer between the evergreens and the aspens turned golden yellow? There is a fascination each of us has when nature paints the countryside with sweeping strokes of color at the changing of the seasons.

Progressing further, we find the importance of color in the animal kingdom. Animals come not only in different shapes and sizes but also in different colors. Yet in the animal kingdom color serves more than merely an ornamental or decorative purpose. Nature is neither chaotic nor random in its selection and use of color. For color in the animal kingdom serves an essential function. The coloring of some animals has importance in their mating. Who has not marvelled at the colors of a peacock, as it struts in courting with feathers fanned? In other animals their coloring blends into the natural surroundings to conceal them from prey and predator alike. The lion is often lost to sight within the tall grass of the African plains, and the deer blends in with the colors of the woods. If these two animals' coloring were different, their ability to survive in their present environments would definitely be affected. Man has taken a cue from the animal kingdom. In order to do battle in guerrilla warfare man has selected for his uniform a coloring that blends into the surroundings.

In our own lives each of us has probably stood in awe as some natural phenomenon unfolded before our eyes. To stand at the ocean's edge and watch the sun rise, as if rising from the ocean to cast diamonds of light across the water at our feet, is a truly breathtaking experience. Or to be in the desert while gray and black storm clouds turn day into night, pierced only by the shrieking streaks of white lightning. To see the sun like a distant burning disk fall into the plains, casting the wheatfields aglow in fiery red. Or to be in the mountains as the weather clears from a summer storm and watch a rainbow bridge two mountain summits. Such colorful spectacles make man realize and appreciate the beauty of life.

Since it affects us most directly, our awareness of color focuses primarily on the daily lighting changes. The absolutes of night and day are so much a part of our lives, we virtually take for granted the gradations of light through the day. While there is no doubt that we are cognizant of a beautiful, sunny day, our awareness is heightened if the beautiful, sunny day follows three or four days of overcast skies. Otherwise, we tend to become oblivious to the infinite shadings of color resulting from natural light. We are used to it. There is no novelty to it. And, thus, we neglect it.

But the lighting and color of our environment during the day is a study of gradations and polarities. Prior to dawn our world is hushed, for nature is at rest. At this stage the two absolutes, black and white, predominate, and there is a shadowless quality to the lighting. As dawn approaches, the world in excited anticipation begins to awaken. Colors grow stronger and differentiate from the absolute polarities of black and white. At sunrise the world breaks forth in splendor. Lighting

13

changes radically. While there is a maintenance of polarity in the contrasts of light and shadow, this polarity has moved away from the absolutes of black and white toward the red-blue polarity. The color of the sun is toward the red end of the spectrum, and the shadows tend toward the blue end. The lighting and coloring at this time of day result from the fact that the sun is shining from the horizon and must penetrate a great amount of atmosphere. As the sun rises farther in the sky, the differentiation of and contrast between colors increases. Until it reaches its zenith, the rising sun increases in its yellow color. Around midday colors are at their sharpest. The sun's light appears white and the shadows black. When the sun starts its descent, the lighting again grows warmer, as it moves back toward the red end of the spectrum. The shadows return to the blue side. At sunset the sun appears as a deep red, for once more it is shining through a great amount of atmosphere. With the setting of the sun the clouds in the sky reflect a multitude of color, until the sun has fallen so far as to leave the world in increasing darkness. The world rests, wrapped in the gray and black of night.

Throughout the day the lighting and color of our environment change, both as a result of the color gradation of lighting from the sun and the contrasting color of the shadows. Yet how many of us have experienced the entire daily progression of the sun? Probably few. For we live a fast-paced life. The time we allow ourselves for observation and receptivity are often momentary snatches from a life consumed in grasping our realities. If we find the time, we enjoy an occasional sunrise and a brief glimpse of the setting sun. Beyond that, we have not got the time. And the same is true of our present appreciation for color. We enjoy color, but we experience it as separate, isolated incidents of spectacle. Too few of us are aware of the use and benefit of color. We relegate color to the realm of the artist.

It is the artist who has mastered color as an expression of his feelings, moods, and thoughts for all to share. The works of such artists as Monet, van Gogh, and Kandinsky have most likely struck a chord in every one of us at some point in time. Their hours of concentrated work in the study of color have given us a testimony to color's effects upon our lives. We build museums in which to hang their works and buy reproductions of their art to decorate our homes. The painter is not, and should not be, the only one who is aware of color. In the world of literature D.H. Lawrence stands out as a man aware of color when he wrote in his short story, "Sun":

> "She was thinking inside herself, of the sun in his splendour, and her mating with him. Her life was now a whole ritual. She lay always awake, before dawn, watching for the grey to colour to pale gold, to know if cloud lay on the sea's edge. Her joy was when he rose all molten in his nakedness, and threw off blue-white fire, into the tender heaven.
> "But sometimes he came ruddy, like a big, shy creature. And sometimes slow and crimson red, with a look of anger, slowly pushing and shouldering. Sometimes again she could not see him, only the level cloud threw down gold and scarlet from above, as he moved behind the wall."

Similar to Lawrence's use of color to establish the mood in his story, our language incorporates phrases of color to express our feelings or describe certain situations. We speak of a jealous person as being green with envy. We watch Western movies and hear the gunslinger challenge a cowboy's courage by calling him a yellow-belly. We feel the blues, and American blacks have long sung the blues. And who has not ended a weekend of fun and relaxation by returning to work on a blue Monday? As if taunted like a bull by the matador's cape, we express our fuming anger as "seeing red." We also describe a city's area of passion as the red-light

15

district. Color permeates our language. Our songs are filled with color. Our lives are nothing, if not colorful. Yet why does color play such a significant role in the description of our feelings?

David Katz, a Gestalt psychologist, studied the importance of color. Katz felt that color was more fundamental than shape in the construction of forms. Postulating a closer relationship between color and emotion than between shape and emotion, Katz devised a test for young children to confirm his hypothesis. In his experiment Katz took the basic shapes of circles, triangles, and squares, and painted three of each shape in one of the three primary colors of red, yellow, and blue. Katz then placed these nine blocks of three different shapes and three different colors before children and asked them to put similar things together. In most cases, the children selected the similar colors as opposed to the similar shapes. Katz had confirmed the validity of the primacy of color in our lives.

Although the importance of color in our lives has been repeatedly shown to us in experiment after experiment, industry has been a major catalyst to increase our awareness of color. Interested in the production, marketing, and sale of its merchandise, industry has used color in the packaging of its products to affect our purchasing decisions and persuade us to buy their particular product. To walk down any supermarket's aisles with the shelves stocked with hundreds of items row upon row is like being in Alice's Wonderland. For the brightly decorated packages in full color virtually scream at us, "Eat Me!", "Drink Me!", "Buy Me!" If we are unconscious to the effects of colors, we'll pick up a package that appeals to us and purchase the product not on the basis of its quality but because of its appearance. The continual improvements in advertising techniques leave the mind dazed. When we watch television on a color set, we see commercials comparable to the imagination and beauty of Disney's *Fantasia*. In fact, commercials are often more visually entertaining than the shows themselves. The improvement in packaging can be seen most readily in the automobile industry. When Henry Ford first manufactured his Model T, the car came in one color—black. Today cars come in a rainbow of colors. Likewise, kitchen appliances are no longer made just in white but afford the housewife a wide range of color assortment in order to coordinate the colors of her kitchen.

Industry also uses color psychology to increase productivity and reduce fatigue among its employees. Although it has been found that people tend to be more lively and active when they work in a red light vibration, they tire easily and are more prone to accidents on the job than if they work under a green light vibration.

Aware of the significance of color to their trade, hotels hire color consultants to design their accommodations with an atmosphere of comfort and pleasure. Could you imagine a bridal suite done in browns, grays, or black? It would provide quite a depressing start to a life of conjugal bliss. Or if we were to fly off to Carnival in Rio de Janeiro, wouldn't we be put off if the airplane's interior was dark and muddy in color? Indeed we would. No airline would dare venture to use murky colors in their planes, unless they were angling for a Chapter 11 filing for bankruptcy. In fact, airlines entice us to fly with them by using light, happy pastel colors in their airplanes. One recently publicized example of this strategy was Braniff airlines' commission of Alexander Calder to design a colorful imprint for the exterior of their planes.

Society's institutions have come to the realization of color's psychology. The medical profession has discovered the use of color to aid their patients' recovery and increase their staff's effectiveness. Walls of hospitals are no longer painted only in dull grays or sterile, glaring whites. To stimulate or cheer a patient suffering from depression or lack of vitality, tones of reds, pinks, and oranges have been successfully employed. To tranquilize and soothe patients with nervous strains or

17

afflicted by hyperactivity, the tones of blues and greens have been used. Even penal institutions have begun to use more color in their facilities. To curb the outbreak of disturbances among the prisoners, authorities have experimented with color and have found that light, pastel shades on the walls help to keep the inmates more composed.

Although fire trucks are generally a bright red, there is a decreasing use of strong, forceful colors on police cars. When the police increasingly came under attack, many police departments sought to change their image from that of an authoritarian keeper of the order to that of protector of community interests. A result of this policy has been to use softer tones on police vehicles. In one large city in the United States, where sniping had threatened the lives of police officers patrolling in department vehicles, the police department changed the color of their patrol cars from red to blue. Sniping decreased after the change.

Schools have begun to use color to achieve the optimum potential in their students. By means of color, educators can increase the concentration of their students, stimulate the level of energy, and reduce eye fatigue. Slow learners are found to improve their skills when placed in yellow-colored rooms.

Today there is greater expression in architecture, more of an attempt to incorporate lighting and color in the construction of a building. No longer are all buildings made of plain red brick. As it reflects in mirror-image the colorful procession of the day, the extensive use of glass gives buildings a chorus of color. In New York and other metropolitan centers artists have taken to the streets to paint the walls of drab buildings with brightly colored murals. All around us the conscious use of color is increasing. No longer does color merely serve a decorative or ornamental function. No longer can color be relegated solely to the artist. For color is an integral part of our lives. It is as fundamental to us as our limbs or the organs of our body. And yet we remain largely ignorant of the benefit to be gained from our conscious use of color.

It is the purpose of this book to make the reader more aware of color, to give you an understanding of the psychological meanings of colors, to offer you techniques by which you can use color to improve your life and your well-being. You may find particularly fascinating the section on the colors that are you. In this section are shown the means to discover the colors that compose your own individual rainbow. Each one of us is different. Each one of us is unique. Some of us are thrilled by colors that repulse others. But no longer need we choose colors by random selection or the whim of the moment. We can consciously select colors to enlighten our spirits and nourish our soul. For as Wassily Kandinsky, the Russian abstract painter, wrote:

"Generally speaking, color directly influences the soul. Color is the keyboard, the eyes are the hammers, the soul is the piano with many strings. The artist is the hand that plays, touching one key after another purposively, to cause vibrations in the soul.

"It is evident therefore that color harmony must rest ultimately on purposive playing upon the human soul; this is one of the guiding principles of internal necessity."

With the words of a master of color as inspiration, let us proceed then to our exploration of the world of color. Awaiting us over the rainbow is a pot of gold, from which each one of us can learn to become a master artist in the art of living. As every journey begins with the first step, let us begin with the consideration of what color really is.

Chapter 2

Scientific Explanations for Color

Man's understanding of the fundamentals of color results primarily from the endeavors of Isaac Newton in the seventeenth century. While investigating ways to improve the telescope, Newton made a discovery that revolutionized man's concept of color. Before Newton's discovery, color was assumed to be an inherent attribute of every material object. Color was contained within the object. However, Newton proved that color was not an inherent attribute of an object but rather the effect of light falling upon the object. Light is the source of color.

Newton's experiment, which so totally changed man's thinking, was undertaken in a darkened room. From a slit in a window shade Newton passed a beam of sunlight through a glass prism. Upon emerging from the prism, the light was no longer a single beam of white light but had dispersed into its elements, the spectrum of the seven rays of color—red, orange, yel-

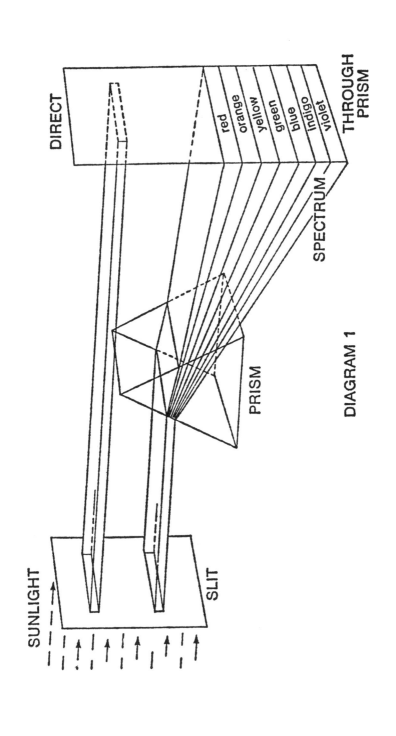

SUNLIGHT

SLIT

DIRECT

THROUGH
PRISM

red
orange
yellow
green
blue
indigo
violet

SPECTRUM

PRISM

DIAGRAM 1

low, green, blue, indigo, violet. (See diagram 1.) As Newton wrote in his book, *Optics:*

> "The Spectrum did appear tinged with this Series of Colours, violet, indigo, blue, green, yellow, orange, red, together with all their intermediate Degrees in a continual Succession perpetually varying. So that there appeared as many Degrees of Colours, as there were sorts of Rays differing in Refrangibility."

Newton had categorically defined the seven-tiered spectrum of color. Prior to Newton, others had worked with prisms and had seen a beam of light broken into many rays. But none had classified the color spectrum, as did Newton. Although Newton believed that color was related to music, his critics derided his seven-color spectrum as an arbitrary attempt to link color with the notes of the diatonic scale. They claimed Newton's spectrum to be the result of his mystical delusions. Totally tied to the materialistic perspective of life, these critics could not allow themselves the open mind of a Newton, and, thus, their lasting significance to the world of science has been something less than Newton's. For science asks the assistance of men and women with the vision of a Newton. Science calls for those who are willing to question impartially the present concepts of knowledge, to test objectively the factors relevant to inquiry, to search constantly for the continual evolution of truth.

If we were to re-create this initial phase of Newton's experiment, we too would discover a spectrum of colors resulting from the beam of white light passed through a glass prism. Like a rainbow the beam of light would break forth into color. Despite the fact that this initial phase of Newton's experiment held much significance for the increased awareness of color, the second phase of his experiment was even more revolutionary. For during this second phase Newton placed a second prism in the path of the light. After the beam of sunlight had passed through the first prism and had dispersed into its component elements of color, this rainbow spectrum was passed through a second prism. Newton may have proceeded with this second stage of the experiment in order to test the prevailing theory relating to the dispersion of light through a prism. For the contemporary thought as to the cause of light breaking into color was that the color was latent in the glass prism and thus "colored" the light rays. If this were so, Newton surmised, then to pass the color rays of light through a second prism would create further dispersion or breaking down into colors. What Newton did find, however, was quite the reverse. Instead of breaking down into further color rays, the rays of light emerging from the second prism reconstructed the beam of sunlight. (See diagram 2.) Newton had passed a beam of light through one prism and had dispersed the light into its spectrum of color. Newton had passed this spectrum of color through another prism and had reconstituted the beam of light. Newton had discovered the source of color. Light contained all color.

But how could a beam of white light break into the seven colors, we might ask? As Newton mentioned in the quotation from *Optics*, the cause was Refrangibility, or what we term Refraction. Light travels at a constant rate of 186,000 miles per second. Yet within this light we have seen the results of dispersion: the color spectrum. We have seven basic colors, each of which has some different characteristic in order to differentiate them one from the other. This different characteristic or quality of differentiation produces different sensations upon the retina of the eye. As a result, we see different colors. Newton understood this phenomenon and stated it in his *Optics:*

"For the Rays to speak properly are not coloured. In them there is nothing else than a certain Power

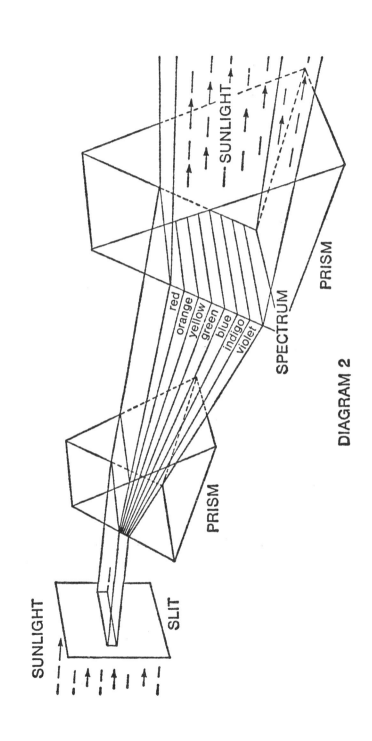

SUNLIGHT

SLIT

PRISM

red
orange
yellow
green
blue
indigo
violet

SPECTRUM

SUNLIGHT

PRISM

DIAGRAM 2

and Disposition to stir up a Sensation of this or that Colour."

And what is this "Power and Disposition" of the rays, as Newton termed it? The different characteristic that results in varying colors is the wavelength of the rays. The waves vary in length, each wavelength being measured as the distance between the crest of any wave and the crest of the following wave. If we were to once again perform the initial phase of Newton's experiment, we would see a sequential order to the arrangement of the colors of the spectrum. Dependent upon the wavelengths of the color rays, the arrangement of the color spectrum will not change. Whenever we pass light through a prism, the resulting color rays are refracted (or bent) as they pass through the medium of the prism. This is true of virtually any medium. For example, if we were to look at an object in a lake from above the water and then were to reach for the object, we would most likely miss it. For the light, upon entering the water, has been refracted. The object will appear farther away than it actually is.

In our color spectrum the long waves are refracted less than the shorter waves. Since red has the longest wavelength of any color visible to the human eye, the red rays would be the least refracted of the color rays. The wavelengths for red light are 8.10^{-5} centimeters (or about 0.8μ [a micron $= 1/1000$ of a millimeter]). At the other end of the color spectrum, violet light has a wavelength of 4.10^{-5} centimeters (or about 0.4μ). The violet rays would be the most refracted of the color rays, followed by indigo, blue, green, yellow, orange, and then red, the least refracted of the color rays.

As we can see from the wavelengths of the violet and red rays, visible light falls within a minuscule range. Within this span are all the colors visible to our eyes. Our eyes function as a means to translate the energy and forces of life into shapes and forms. These forms and shapes appear in a myriad of colors, for the variance in the wavelengths of the rays affects our visual faculties and creates the sensation we call color.

If color is not an inherent characteristic of a material object, how does an object partake of a certain color? How does a specific item appear to us as red, green, blue, or any other color? By means of the process of absorption and reflection. In this dual process we have all the elements of coloration. Consider the absolutes of light—white and black. Although we may have been taught that white and black are colors, in actuality they represent the polarities of light and darkness. Newton proved white light contains all color. Conversely, black is the negation of all color, or the absence of light. Although this is the reality of white and black, the two "colors," as we often term them, are used in the coloring of our clothes, our furniture, our material possessions. Perhaps through these two "colors" we can best understand the process of absorption and reflection. For in black is the total absorption of all colors and in white the total reflection of all color.

Anyone who has been dressed in black on a sweltering summer day can relate to the absorptive quality of black. For the experience seems similar to what the sensation of being roasted alive must feel like. It's unbearable. Consequently, we should not be surprised that summer wardrobes tend toward the lighter colors, while during the winter our clothes assume darker colors. Almost like a chameleon we change our apparel's coloring according to the climate. In our use of color for painted surfaces we find no paint reflects more light than white, nor less than black. In considering the "real" colors, the colors of our spectrum, we find the colors toward the red end of the spectrum are more closely related to black. The colors toward the violet end of the spectrum are more closely associated with white. This fact can be understood by the wavelengths of the two color rays at the ends of the spectrum. As we mentioned above, the violet end of the spectrum has shorter wavelengths. Violet light vibrates

27

more rapidly and approaches greater energy than do the color rays toward the red end with their longer wavelengths. As a result, violet is more aligned to the pure energy of white light, while red is more aligned to the heavier, weightier "energy" of black light. Objects of red color absorb more light than will an object of a violet color.

In this process of absorption and reflection, we return again to the basics of color. When light hits the surface of an object, some of the colors are absorbed within the object. The only colors visible to us are those reflected back. For instance, an apple absorbs most colors, except red. Therefore, the color of the apple will appear to us as red. Light strikes different objects and projects to our visual perception certain colors. The color of the object we see is the color reflected by the object, all other color rays having been absorbed by the object itself. In the sunset we see a process similar to reflection-absorption. In this case, however, absorption becomes a dispersion or scattering of certain color rays. As in the case of absorption and reflection, we find the rays of the violet end of the spectrum with their shorter wavelengths to be more readily dispersed than those of the red end of the spectrum with their longer wavelengths. As the sun progresses from its midday zenith, it is seen in its descent through more and more of the atmosphere until it reaches the horizon, at which point the sunlight is penetrating the maximum atmosphere. At sunset we see the sun as a distant red disk. The shorter wavelengths of color have been scattered out of the direct rays of the light by their absorption into the atmosphere. These colors are eliminated, and the red of the sun predominates. Light seeks a balance, as does life. We can see this in the process of absorption and reflection, and we can see it in the idea of light and dark. In the previous chapter we mentioned the sun's progression through the day and the change in the lighting and shadows of the day. We spoke of the morning and evening lighting as being of a red quality with the shadows taking on blue tones. We pointed out the appearance of the sun as white light at midday, while the shadows cast are black. The duality in light and in coloration has been seen through the phenomenon of absorption—reflection. In the next chapter we shall deal more fully with this necessary duality in life. For life is energy, pure and simple. Because of this constant blending of forces and energies, different manifestations occur both in form and in coloration.

Among the critics of Newton's seven-tiered spectrum have been those who stress three primary colors as the requisite colors from which all other colors can be produced. Prior to 1731, J.C. Le Blon advocated a color trinity of red, yellow, and blue as the primary colors. Others who have endorsed this color triad include Goethe, M.E. Chevreul, Arthur Pope, and Walter Sargent. Although proposed by Le Blon, this primary system is known as the Brewsterian system, after Sir David Brewster. Another group has contended that the primary colors are not red, yellow, and blue but rather the color trinity of red, green, and violet. In relation to Newton's seven-colored spectrum this color triad contains the two extremes of Newton's spectrum and the middle color of green. In this controversy over primary colors, however, let us remember color is a sensation upon our faculties of sight. Our perception of color is dependent upon our eyes. In 1802 Thomas Young described the retina of the eye as having three systems of reception, each of which responds to one of the three primary colors of red, green, and violet. One system of reception responds primarily to the red end of the spectrum, another to the violet end, and the third to the middle green. Young's recognition of the systems of color reception in the eye led to his advocacy of the three primary colors being red, green, and violet. This color triad was later supported by James Clerk Maxwell and Hermann von Helmholtz and eventually became known as the Young-Helmholtz three-components theory.

The process of three is fundamental to the effectiveness of our visual faculties. Parallel to the triad of primary colors and the three systems of color reception in the retina, the dynamics of our sight are revealed by an analogy to electronics' basic threefold process of transmission—reception—and the interval between. While our eyes receive impressions from a source, there is always the possibility of distortion in the reception of these impressions. If the receivers in our eyes are impaired, we might be afflicted by astigmatisms, resulting in shortsightedness, farsightedness, color deficiency, or even blindness. The result, needless to say, is an inability of the eyes to perceive clearly the impressions reaching us. Another potential for distortion occurs in the interval between transmission and reception. For instance, if we were driving along a road, we might be able to see a road sign clearly from 100 yards distance. But if it were foggy on that same road, our ability to see the road sign could definitely be affected. At sunset our perception of the color of the sun changes radically because of the interval between the sun and where we stand, the interval in this case being the atmospheric pressure.

When we discuss the interval between transmission and reception, we should speak of the means of traversing the distance of space-time coordinates to arrive at the receiver from the source. In our case of light we understand light to travel at 186,000 miles per second. But how does light travel? This is a question that has long perplexed scientists. Two opposing theories have vied for predominance until the recent attempt to synthesize the two.

At virtually the same time in the seventeenth century, Isaac Newton and the Dutch mathematician Christiaan Huygens proposed two contrary theories on the character of light and light transmission. Newton's theory, known as the Corpuscular Theory, conceives of light as being rays composed of extremely small particles. Light is seen as a "thing," material corpuscles projected through space in straight lines. Although Newton's influence gave prominence to the Corpuscular Theory during the eighteenth century, Newton's theory eventually gave way to the concept of the Wave Theory. Although aware of the Wave Theory as proposed by Huygens, Newton could not accept its explanation for the character of light. For the Wave Theory, in simplistic terms, sees light as a "process" similar to the rippling of waves across a body of water's surface. In the rippling of waves there is some sideward motion. If light were a wave phenomena, Newton suggested, then there would be a spreading of the light and some loss of light associated with it. The facts contradicted such a possibility, he asserted, for light travels with little loss to either side. Yet in the length of the waves of visible light, we resolve Newton's contention. Experiments have shown that the smaller the length of the wave compared to the width of the wave, the smaller the sideward spreading becomes. Remember in our wavelengths of light we are dealing with an incredibly rapid process and infinitesimally small quantities. Therefore, any spreading would go unnoticed by our visual perception.

Considering light as a vibration comparable to the vibration of sound, Huygens proposed the Pulse Theory, the forerunner of the Wave Theory. To Huygens and the wave theorists light is a "process" and not a "thing," as in Newton's Corpuscular Theory. Huygens assumed the existence of minute particles totally filling space. Termed *aether*, these particles were initially considered the necessary medium for the transference of light. A disturbance of the aether, light is viewed as a transmission of shocks from aetheric particle to aetheric particle. As the light moves from particle to particle, it assumes a continuous wave-like disturbance. From its source the light, like the rippling waves on a body of water, spreads out in ever-increasing circles. But unlike the waves of water, which primarily rise and fall, the waves of light have no such specific direction and can move either from side to side, up or down, or some direction between the two. Although we have mentioned Newton's basis for contention against the validity of the Wave Theory, let us see why Newton's Corpuscular Theory proved untenable.

According to Newton's Corpuscular Theory, if two rays of light are brought together to meet at one point, then we would presume additional brightness as the result. We would expect this additional brightness to be equivalent to the sum of all the light particles. While this is often valid, it is also possible to have quite the reverse effect: that is, an increase of darkness. Newton's theory can not explain such an effect, but the Wave Theory can. If we assume the ray of light to move as a wave, then we can attribute the polarities of positive and negative to the crest and the trough of the wave. Therefore, when the wave crest of one light ray meets the wave crest of another light ray, the light is intensified in brilliance. But should the wave crest of one light ray meet the wave trough of another light ray, they cancel each other out and extinguish the brightness of the rays. This phenomenon was theoretically proposed by Thomas Young and given foundation by Augustin Jean Fresnel. Interference, as this phenomenon is called, led to the acceptance of the Wave Theory as the explanation for the character of light (wavelengths) and the transmission of light. Although the Wave Theory gained dominance in the nineteenth century, the twentieth century was to see another theory come to the fore.

In 1900 Max Planck seemed to revive Newton's Corpuscular Theory by introducing the atom into the concept of energy. In any exchange between electrical waves and material substance, Planck stated, the energy of the electrical waves takes atomic form. Planck termed this atom of energy as the energy quantum, from which arose the Quantum Theory. As a result of his work on the photo-electric effect, Albert Einstein in 1905 advanced Planck's theories by postulating light quanta (termed photons) as comparable to energy quanta. Einstein declared the photon to be energy and not merely a carrier of energy. Einstein described light waves as needle-like structures. He claimed that light is not a process of radiation to all sides but rather is similar to a flashlight, radiating in a narrow beam. This radiation is momentary, resulting in light emission travelling through space as an impulse of packets of energy.

Unfortunately, Einstein was not able to explain away the phenomena of diffraction and interference, both of which corroborate the validity of the Wave Theory. Therefore, at this point in time we consider light to have dual aspects: at times light behaves like a wave and at other times like a particle. Light is neither completely a wave, nor completely a particle, but seems to be a wave-particle (wavicle). Eventually, scientists may prove the process of light to be only one more validation of the duality of matter. For as science advances man's knowledge, the basic truths of ancient wisdom are continually confirmed. Although accused by materialistic-mired scientists as fabrications or delusions of spiritualism and mysticism, these truths have been handed down to mankind through the mystery teachings of the Egyptians, the Pythagorean thought of the Greeks, the Jewish energy system of the Qabalah, and Christianity's Bible. In the following chapter we shall deal with some of these occult truths and their relation to certain concepts outlined in this chapter.

Chapter 3

The Spiritual Aura of Color

So involved is our specialized society in the inspection and analysis of small, separated niches of reality that we lose sight of the whole, of the totality of existence. Even our explorers in the realm of human knowledge, scientists, often lose themselves to a mere extension of the past without vision or foresight of the transitory limits of man's understanding of life. For while life is a procession of evolving thought and knowledge, there are times when catalytic changes rise to the fore and challenge man to depart from his routine, to accelerate the unfolding of his understanding, to face the actual experience of life and abandon his devised fantasies of life. At this point in time (1977), man is reaching such a period. Based upon opinions and subjective expectations, many of man's concepts are no longer relevant to the reality of his present experience. The institutions he has constructed for security and meaning are found wanting and are crumbling from decay. If mankind is to make the transition from the past into the present, we must all become aware of the realities of our existence. No longer can our fixed, static beliefs about life be relied upon, for they must give way to the recognition of continual change in life and an acceptance of the Einsteinian universe with its integration of the three coordinates of space and the dimension of time.

Prior to the verbalization of relativity, man believed life to be broken into finite periods of existence. Space—time were dissected. Any situation was seen as a definite, singular incident, contained within a certain time period. The initiating causes of the incident were neglected, as were the subsequent effects of the incident. Man had separated time from space. The man of science assumed an experiment carried out at one point in time to hold total validity at another point in time. The man of government built a society where precedent was the answer to the future. The man of learning relied upon the security of experience for his knowledge. The continual change in the cycles of life was forgotten. Man allowed himself a period of stagnation. And the result? Is it necessary to enumerate? All we need do is to look around us. Man is at war with himself. He fights his brothers with the vengeance of the savage. Living a life of frustration and misery, he seeks placebos in the escape valves of drugs, alcohol, conquest, and destruction. Yet change is a continual phenomenon and as such a constant source of hope. Man can change, if he wills to do so.

In the last chapter we saw the evolution of man's knowledge regarding the transmission and character of light. Does not the change in belief from one theory to another offer us the reality to the statement that what might be true at one point in time may be totally invalid at another point in time? While our knowledge at one specific time might give credence to one viewpoint, man's exploration beyond the limits of his present knowledge can eventually lead to greater understanding of reality. In order for us to regain what could be a paradise on earth and to eliminate the agony and despair of life, we must be ever open and receptive to new thoughts, changing knowledge, and the insistence of vision. We must dispense with our anticipations and expectations based upon wrong modes of thought.

Let us remember that our species is differentiated from other life forms on this earth by the mental faculties inherent in us. By the use of reason we have the ability to exercise free-will or choice, rather than being totally run by our instincts or controlled by our past realities. However, we can only use this faculty intelligently if we will re-educate our minds and increase our awareness of our being. In order to develop our self-respect we need to clean out the garbage cluttering our minds, garbage heaped upon us by the restraints of an educational process and a society lost from the direction of reality in the maze of established yet antiquated concepts.

Not only must we continue to investigate the experiences of life for greater insight, but we must now relate the parts to the whole. Let us not lose sight of the totality of reality, for otherwise we shall remain ensnared in the traps of our wrong thinking, our frustrations, and our despair. Should you think I have presented an overly pessimistic view of our present mode of existence, let me assure you there are always branches by which the individual can pull himself out of his own life's mess. And it is the individual who must perform such a task. For who else can do the job for him? Can we rely upon our educators, our politicians, our religious leaders? Or will each of us take the reins of responsibility and decide to stand like men? Our evolution to greater self-awareness can come only through our willingness to struggle persistently in behalf of the goal. Unlike some forms of breakfast foods, coffees, or gratifications, there is no such thing as instant enlightenment, even though we see some self-appointed teachers like circus barkers claiming to have the Answer. Any intelligent person who jumps on the carousel of "spiritual" institutions may soon find himself jumping from one pony of spiritual teachings to another pony in order to grab the brass ring of self-awareness. Eventually, the seeker must jump off this carousel of psychedelic delights and realize—there is no instant solution. There is no immediate satisfaction. At least of a lasting nature. Like the farmer who laboriously works his fields, those in search of increased self-understanding must diligently sow their fields of consciousness with the seeds of truth. In this sowing process we must allow the necessary time factor for the seeds to gestate, to germinate, to eventually grow stronger and bear us the fruit of our labors. Let us not forget the subtle truth to the Biblical phrase, "As ye sow, so shall ye reap."

As the farmer receives yearly seed catalogues, mankind has been offered an assortment of seeds to plant in his consciousness and to spur his quest for understanding and inner peace. We find these seeds in the systems we call the Gnosis (wisdom). They are universal seeds and have been found with the regional flavorings of the ancient Egyptian teachings, the wisdom of the Greeks and Pythagoras, the examples of Gautama Buddha and Zoroaster, the teachings of the Christ, the energy system of the Qabalah, the writings of such as Whitman, the music of Wagner—wherever man has strived to realize the spark of divinity within himself. Many are the outlets available to educate ourselves in the reality of life. If we will look at these systems objectively and with discrimination, we will find the benefit they offer to re-educate our minds and return us to the direction of reality, to the Garden of Eden. Let each of us begin to sow our fields with right living, true understanding, and a compassion for the plight of our brothers. While the process of evolution is an individual one, so too is it a process of the totality.

As we shall deal later in the book with the use of numerology and color as a means to self-analysis and increased well-being, let us consider the universal significance of three numbers with which we dealt in the last chapter. These numbers are the number two, which we saw in the process of absorption-reflection and contrast of light-dark; the number three, which revealed the dynamics of our color reception both by the process of color primaries and by our visual organs; and the number seven, which we found to be the spectrum of color.

When we consider the significance of the number two, we are dealing with the primal division expressed in the statement of the ancients: "From the one to the many." For from the unity of the one, from the gestalt or totality of existence, differentiation occurs. The initial separation is into the two, representative of the duality in nature. In life we find there are two primary poles: the positive and the negative. Both are essential to life. When the spark of life is ignited, a force is projected into being. The active, positive force needs a form and acquires the passive, negative receptivity in the containment of energy. Energy seeks form. Yet within every life form is energy, for without a continuation of the active, positive principle of life the form would stagnate and die. There can be no life without energy. If we think of the batteries used in our cars and flashlights, we can recognize the necessity for a connection between the two poles, the energy contained within the battery cannot manifest itself and remains latent.

The polarity in nature can be seen in movement with its dual phase of action and reaction. Action serves as the propelling force, acting upon some thing. Action is the initiating force. Reaction is the movement generated by the active force. Reaction is the form of response to action. Should either phase prove functionally inoperative, we are dealing with an unbalanced situation that must eventually give way to destructive consequences.

In our own lives we realize the need to alternate activity with rest. For example, if we have a project due on a certain date and find ourselves pressed for time, we might push ourselves to complete the task without allowing adequate time for rest or sleep. The reaction? Anyone who has done a term paper in school or college at the last minute knows the feeling. In the jargon of the student, the feeling upon completion of the paper is one of being totally wasted. Having so completely run our batteries down, we are not functioning at our optimum but rather at a low level of energy. If we continue at such a pace for an extended period of time, our vitality suffers, and our bodies must give way to increasing forms of disease and ill-health. To maintain our health and a state of balance we must seek rhythmic alternation in our life patterns. Otherwise, disequilibrium is set into motion with its consequent effects of ill-health.

As life demands the balance of polarity, we can become more aware of this balancing act in the process of rhythmic alternation. In daily life we note this alternation with the dawning of the day, when there is much activity and positive exertion, and with the settling of the night, when the world rests and activity is latent. Alternation is demonstrated in the tidal systems of our oceans with their incoming and outgoing tides and in the movement of the waves with their crests and troughs. We saw this wave movement in our consideration of light transmission and the phenomenon of interference, where light will increase or decrease when two waves of light meet according to whether the point of contact is at the crests of both waves or at the crest of one and trough of the other. This alternative process is evident, as well, in our symbol for infinity, ∞. This symbol reveals an understanding of life as a continual alternation between the positive and the negative, between the objective and subjective arcs of existence, between evolution (the outward development of a being or system) and involution (the inward development).

In physics we find the positive and negative forces in the form of centrifugal and centripetal force. In centrifugal force we have a rotating part being pulled off its rotational orbit around the center to fly off at a

40

tangent. To maintain the equilibrium of rotational movement there must be a countervailing force, which we call centripetal force. Acting in a manner opposite to the centrifugal force, centripetal force pulls the rotating part toward the center. For proper operation of this rotational movement a balance between the centrifugal and centripetal forces must be arrived at. Let us use the concept of these two forces in reflecting upon the order of our solar system. If it were not for some degree of balance between the centrifugal and centripetal forces, our solar system would either fly apart with planets thrown out into distant, remote portions of space away from their natural spatial coordinates, resulting in possible destruction, or at the very least, radical transformations of energy; or on the other hand, as some fatalistic futurists predict, the planets of our solar system would be sucked one by one into the sun, the center of our system. Within the duality of nature it is essential for a balance to be struck. Without an integrating, mediating influence we would merely have the polarity of extremes without connection or synthesis.

In our description of absorption and reflection we observed a process similar to centrifugal and centripetal force. As we mentioned in the preceding chapter, our perception of color results from certain rays of light being reflected, while the other rays of light are absorbed within the object. Absorption parallels centripetal force with rays being taken within the object. Reflection parallels centrifugal force with rays being repulsed from the core of the object. We also have this duality in the contrast of the absolutes of light. As we discussed in the work of Isaac Newton, in white we have all-light, containing the entire spectrum of color. In black we have the negation of light, or a total absorption of color. To make this concept more relevant to our daily lives, we need only recall our examples of the absorption of the summer sun's rays into a black

41

suit and the reflection of light on painted surfaces being at its maximum with "white" paint.

We can relate our absolutes of white and black to energy as well. In white we have the active forces of life. White light represents the positive polarity of action and energy of the day. White is stimulating and reflective. On the other hand, black is absorptive. In black is the passive energy of life, the darkness and recuperation of the night. In our spectral range of color we discovered the wavelengths toward the violet end of the spectrum to be more rapid, and, in a sense, containing more energy. The wavelengths toward the red end of the spectrum were seen to be slower and perhaps "heavier." Approaching greater energy than does the red end of the spectrum, violet is more akin to white, while red is more akin to black. As we continue in our discussion of color, it will be seen that according to spiritual teachings the colors toward the violet end of the spectrum are spiritually uplifting and the colors toward the red end are more physically weighted. In a spiritual sense white represents revelation. In the ancient wisdom we learn of man's attempt through his trials of evolvement to reach ultimately the white light. In spiritual teachings we hear of black magic, where the truths of wisdom are concealed or used improperly to exploit others. Even in our language we have incorporated a subjective use of the terms "white" and "black." In our Western movies the hero usually wears the white hat while the villain is dressed in black. Can you imagine the psychological traumas each of us might go through should the hero appear totally in black and the villain completely in white? When we speak of good and bad, we imagine white to be as "chaste as the driven snow" and black to be the conjuring up of evils and sins. Even though our societal terms have given a subjective perspective to the "colors" white and black, let us remember white and black as two objective realities—white, representing the positive, masculine, active force, and black, the negative, feminine,

42

receptive form. When we think of our subjective use of objective phenomena, is it not interesting that we have confused these two basic polarities in our minds, so that our society emphasizes the white force as opposed to working a balance between the two? Is it not interesting to note the sublimation in most societies of the feminine form to the masculine force? Consider the use of the trinity in Christian theology. While the Father, Son and Holy Ghost are represented in the Trinity, what happened to the mother? What has resulted from our culture's overemphasis of the positive pole? We know for a fact that our focus solely on the red ray of the spectrum could lead to feverish conditions and inflammations. Likewise on the opposite end of the spectrum, concentration on the violet ray might lead to increasing disorganization and a breakdown of the mental faculties. But look around you and note the effects of our total focus on the positive pole.

Do we not find ourselves totally outer-directed, to borrow the term of sociologist David Reisman? Our efforts in life are predominantly exterior-concerned, materially directed. Until the recent emergence of spiritual cults, inner yearnings and women's liberation, Western society had totally emphasized the material conquest of life. Successfully, to a degree. Yet our present state of affairs still finds us overwhelmed by the material aspects of life. As a result of this imbalance between the inner and the outer, our culture's health is suffering. No longer do we construct, we destroy. No longer do we create, we conquer. No longer do we live for today, we die every day. Resulting from our perversion of the functioning of these two opposite forces, we live in an imbalanced society, unable to weight evenly the dual poles of nature.

In certain of man's physiological systems we view the duality in nature. Within man the life process of metabolism is operating at all times. The metabolism is composed of the two forces of anabolism and catabolism. Anabolism serves the functions of building up and repairing the organism, while catabolism eliminates waste products from the organism. To maintain good health and rhythmic living, this dual process must maintain a balance. Either extreme of anabolism or catabolism can lead to disease and ill health. When we take nourishment into our bodies, we transform the ingested substance into energy for our system to assimilate. During this refinement process of assimilation there is an elimination of those parts non-essential to the energy transformation. Waste products must be eliminated from our system, or we accumulate toxins unacceptable to our body's use and well-being.

Apart from the metabolism with its dual functions, man has two nervous systems. One is called the involuntary nervous system, for it automatically operates the functions of the body necessary to the maintenance of life—the pulsation of the heart to stimulate the flow of circulatory fluids, the movements of the digestive system to maintain the balanced metabolism, the expansion and contraction of our lungs for breathing. The other nervous system, termed the voluntary nervous system, is centered on the brain, the spinal cord, and solar plexus. This system is controlled by our conscious direction and results in our capability to think, feel, and act.

Man's brain is divided into the duality of the left and right hemispheres. The left hemisphere of the brain represents the positive force in man and is the foundation for man's electrical force. The right hemisphere represents the negative force in man and is the foundation for man's magnetic nature. When the nerves from the brain enter into the body, the neural wiring crosses. Therefore, in the body the left hemisphere of the brain controls the right side of the body and the right hemisphere of the brain controls the left side of the body.

Alternation can be seen in man's respiratory process. Just as the tides come in and go out, so too does man inhale and exhale in his breathing process. Analogous to the metabolism of the individual with the building up of the organism and the elimination of waste from the organism, in our breathing we take in the life force as we inhale and release certain toxins in our exhalation. Later in this book we shall deal with certain esoteric forms of self-health. One of these forms of self-health is the consciousness focused upon the breathing process. When we breath in, we should try to avoid merely grasping for air and life support but with awareness and rhythmic balance should recognize that in our inhalation we are drawing in not only air but the life force contained within the air. In our exhalation our systems benefit if we are conscious of the elimination of certain waste products. Almost any one who has sat in a reflective, introspective mood and concentrated on rhythmic, deep breathing can attest to the increased relaxation and inner peace within themselves as a result.

We have mentioned the alternation of the day between daylight's positive, active phase and evening's negative, receptive phase. In man it is necessary to be active and passive, to act and react, to do and to rest. A system gaining popularity at present is the theory of biorhythms. In biorhythms three phases of man's being are divided into the alternating cycles of positive (active, outgoing) and negative (passive, absorbing). Seen as charges and discharges of energy, these cycles are viewed in terms of man's physical, sensitivity, and intellectual rhythms. The physical rhythm depicts man's physical energy. On the positive arc or ascending phase the individual feels more robust and energetic than when on the descending arc, the period of recharging and recouping the energy. The sensitivity rhythm affects man's emotional being and can indicate periods of susceptibility to optimism or depression. The intellectual rhythm influences man's mental faculties, affecting the ability of his mind to understand new concepts.

In the wisdom teachings man is understood to be composed of both the positive and negative aspects of nature. In each man and in each woman are both the masculine and feminine factors. These teachings indi-

45

cate that a person's corporeal body, whether masculine or feminine, is the opposite of the inner self of that person. In other words, a person who has a man's body has the feminine attributes of nature inside him. With a woman the body is feminine but the inner self is masculine. Perhaps all of us are aware of experiences where a man presents himself as an image of the ultimate in masculinity. When pushed to his limits, such an individual has a tendency to either flail out uncontrollably at the obstacles to his way or to fold under increasing pressure like a deck of cards. Women, generally speaking, appear delicate, passive, feminine on the outside. But each of us can probably recall incidents demonstrative of the inner strength of woman. In woman is the ability to endure, to tenaciously preserve, to sacrifice if need be. The internal courage of woman is parallel to the external courage of man. The external femininity of woman parallels the internal passivity of man. And a balance must again be struck. One mode of balance is through the function of sexual intercourse. By means of an intimate relationship between man and woman, each is balanced and made whole. The positive force of man's exterior being is soothed by the positive force of woman's inner self. The negative form of man's inner self finds comfort in the negative form of woman's external being. If the man and woman involved in relationship are aware of the fulfillment they give to one another, the sexual act is a process of indescribable beauty. But the key word is awareness. Without the awareness of the compensatory process involved in sexual intercourse, the beauty of true love can degenerate into an animal act of lustful passion, the sharing of love reduced to the subtle conquest of the loved one. To reduce the intercourse of the sexes to an objective statement of function, the similarity is again drawn to the two poles of the car battery. By linking the two poles connection is made. The spark is ignited. Man is electric, woman magnetic, and together they complete the balance between duality to realize totality.

There are two other basic aspects to man's being which we have touched upon just now. Man is made up of both the material and the spiritual. We are all familiar with the material, for our society has overly concentrated on this form for such a long time. This material aspect interests man in form. Consider our own individual quests for material goods. Whatever we may believe is our motivation in the acquisition of possessions, it relates all to one thing: security. We acquire material needs in order to survive. We acquire material wants in order to both appreciate ourselves and to be appreciated by others. However, as we are learning through the pain of experience, this constant accumulation of material possessions does not satisfy an inner craving. Now coming to the force of the consciousness, this inner yearning is the spiritual aspect of man. The spiritual aspect is the positive force in man, the true motivating power for his survival. In reality man is in continual quest to develop his qualities, to evolve his being. Anyone familiar with the Tarot system can see this process in the fall of the fool into the mire of material existence. Biblically viewed, the fall of man represents this same concentration upon the material with the sight lost to the spiritual. The essence of each one of us (the essential part of us under all our garments, skins, psychological tape loops, et cetera, ad nauseam), this essential self is born into material circumstances in order to transmute certain base qualities. This process was called the transmutation of base metal into gold by the alchemists. The alchemists were not concerned with the material transmutation of metal into metal, but were interested in the transmutation of the material into the spiritual—a transmutation similar to the Christ being born in the manger, the stable of animal passions, and rising above such circumstance to realize the golden spark of divinity within, to become the Son of God. When we reflect upon man's long-

47

neglected spirituality, we realize that our corporeal forms are but one pole of duality, the other pole being force.

Each of us has a tendency to assume our perspective of reality to be reality itself. Such an idea is similar to the colors of the world as seen by someone whose systems of color reception are afflicted. Dependent upon our own astigmatisms, each of us views the world according to our own perspective. However, are we seeing clearly? Or is it possible that what appears to be reality is sometimes an illusion? Recent scientific advances give validity to the fact that appearance often differs from the substance or reality of a situation. Realize that we are moving from a universe of separated, finite incidents into the four-dimensional continuum of process in the Einsteinian world. Through physics we are learning life forms are energy patterns manifesting in certain shapes and forms. Through Kirlian photography and the Kilner screen we can understand there is more to the physical body than meets the eye. For example, in Kirlian photography, if we were to take a picture of a leaf on a tree, our photograph would show not only the physical form of the leaf as we perceive it through our eyes but would show a misty periphery to the leaf depicting the energy emanating from that leaf. If one of us were to stand before a Kilner screen, the person concentrating on that screen might see a misty outline over the periphery of the body. This outline has been called the aura or the etheric double. A less confusing term seems appropriate, and, therefore, we could call such energy emanation the electric body. The electric body is the radiation of the energy contained within the physical body. When someone talks about the "good vibes" of another, he is revealing an unconscious knowledge of a basic truth. When we are with other people, we do not merely touch them physically, but our electric body of energy contacts their electric body. Each of us emanates frequencies, but these frequencies are different for each different individual. The closer we are to another, the more entwined our electric bodies become. Recall those experiences in the past when you met someone for the first time. Perhaps you were impressed by them and enjoyed their company. Or maybe you found them to be rather unappealing. There was something about them you just didn't like. Although you couldn't put your finger on it, you were conscious that something about them turned you off. In this latter case the intertwining frequencies between the two of you were in friction and creating a discordant situation. With people we like there is a frequency rapport. In man not only is there the corporeal form but the positive force of the electrical body. Again we see the constant duality in nature.

The need for a means of balance, a connective link, between the two polarities gives us the number three. The number three serves as a mediating force between masculine and feminine aspects in nature. As we have mentioned above, the active, positive principle represents energy and seeks a form in the passive, negative principle. This interaction of these two opposites is reconciled by a third element, serving as the catalyst for the balance. The third factor, the agent of reconciliation, can be seen in the structure of the atom and the influence of the neutron in the atom. For it is the neutron that serves as the binding power, as the regulating influence, between the positive proton and the negative electron. As with the neutron, the third term in a triad is neither active nor passive but rather the neuter or mathematical principle, relating the two other principles to one another. By means of the third factor there is harmonization and completion. For in three we arrive at the first perfect geometrical figure, the triangle. The triangle symbolizes the first figure that completely encloses a space. A point seems to have no such limits, nor does the straight line, which when extended unrestricted continues infinitely. But the triangle formation enforces a boundary to the infinitude.

In three we arrive at the dynamics of process. Although we have the duality of nature in the two forces of positive-negative, it is through three that we move these forces first into reconciliation and then into action. Representing process, three is the first number with beginning, middle, end. It represents flow, the sequential phases inherent in any behavioral process. Consider in your own mind the following examples of this three-fold process:

birth —	life —	death
man	woman	child
seed	germination	plant
childhood	manhood	old age
cause	time	effect
voltage	resistance	current
thesis	antithesis	synthesis
center	radius	circumference
structure	function	order
past	present	future

In order to further draw out the idea of activity associated with three, let us look briefly at the last of these examples: past — present — future. As the Greek philosopher Heraclitus intimated, our lives are like rivers. To support his view of the relativity of life, of the continual process of change in life, Heraclitus offered an analogy of a river. If he were to throw a stone into a river, Heraclitus asserted, he could never throw another stone into that same river. For the river could never be the same as, or identical to, the river into which the stone was thrown. First, it should be understood that the water of the river into which he threw the stone is now farther downstream. "New water," so to speak, fills the spatial coordinates of the river at that second point in time. But even to attempt to stop the river by damming it to points in time is to break up the continuum of the reality of the river. For the reality of the river is a continuous flow of water, of which time is an integral and essential factor to the three spatial coordinates. Secondly, we must consider what objects have intruded the spatial coordinates of the river during the time interval that has transpired between the initial stone-throwing episode and the time of his contemplation as to whether he could throw another stone into the "same" river. The most obvious, of course, is the stone that Heraclitus has thrown into the river. By itself the stone has changed the spatial coordinates of the river. If he were to throw another stone into the river, the spatial coordinates would again change because of the addition of another stone. But there are far more subtle possibilities, infinite in scope. Perhaps several fish have intruded the spatial coordinates for a period as they make their way downstream. Debris from upstream has possibly entered the spatial coordinates of the river. The variables over time are limitless. Yet they are also essential to our consideration of the river and afford us the realization that the river at one point in time is not, and never can be, the same river at another point in time.

The same is true of ourselves. We live in a continual process of growth or decay. Who we are today is not the exact same person as who we were yesterday. We have lived through another day's experiences, each one of which must be different from any other previous experience, even if only to some minute degree. In reality we live in the present. But in our minds too often we live either in the past or in the future. There are those people who constantly relive the happier days of their imagined past, holding on to a security of yesterdays. And there are those people who anticipate the future, living in expectation of better days. But too few live in reality. For the reality of today is today. What you do today is to lay the groundwork for tomorrow. What you did yesterday is seeing some effect in what you do today. This concept has been bandied about recently in the term "karma." People speak of "good" karma and "bad" karma. Too often they don't understand the truth of karma. Karma relates to the

51

law of cause and effect. What you set into motion by your actions will eventually have some effect in your life. What you did in the past is being projected into the present, and what you do in the present will be projected into the future. Let us again remember the Biblical phrase, "As ye sow, so shall ye reap." This simple statement sums up the law of karma. If you choose to live in a world of deceit, dishonesty, and moral lassitude, then prepare yourself to suffer at the hands of your own acts. You may find that your ways will reverberate with severe retaliation. This process is akin to the process of electronics. In electronics we transmit frequencies from a source. These frequencies travel through the spatial coordinates to a receiver. If your mind is filled with clutter and garbage, you will unconsciously be transmitting much of your state of being out to your environment and your surroundings. For just as our physical energy emanates out from our physical body in the form of the electric body, so too do our thoughts and mental state of being transmit out. Some of us know people who seem rather unbalanced in their life rhythms. They have lost awareness and have no idea where they are going or where they are coming from. The lack of harmony in their lives has affected them to such a degree that they unconsciously transmit out their confused states of being. The consequence? These people cannot be depended upon to see any one thing through to its conclusion. Either they get tired of the effort needed to complete the task and give up bitterly frustrated, or they are unable to integrate the parts that go into the making of the whole. Such people are unable to order their energies into a functional structure and, therefore, must project confusion.

The importance of three can be seen in man's physical organs of the ears and the eyes. Our sense of hearing results from the functioning of our ear mechanism, to which there are three sections. These three sections to the ear are known as the external, middle, and internal ears. Within the inner ear are three semicircular canals, arranged in three planes each at right angles to the other two. These semicircular canals afford us the sense of balance. Living on a physical plane with three dimensions of spatial coordinates—length, width, height —we find the need to be able to navigate these three coordinates of space. By means of the fluid inside the semicircular canals we can do so. Should the fluid inside these canals be disturbed, our sense of balance is thrown off. While most animals have similar devices for balance within their ears, it is interesting to note that birds in which these semicircular canals have been removed lose all sense of balance and direction.

In the preceding chapter we discussed the retina of the eye and the three systems of color reception in the retina. To reiterate, each of these systems responds to different parts of the color spectrum. One system responds to the red end, another to the violet end, and the third to the middle green. For a true perspective of color it is necessary that each of these three systems of color reception be functioning in the organism, otherwise the individual is afflicted with color deficiency or even color blindness.

In discussing the concept of the triad of color, we now realize color has two sets of primary colors. Not only does the Young-Helmholtz three-components theory give validity to the triad of spectral light being composed of red, green, and violet; but in painting colors we have the three primaries of red, yellow, and blue, advocated by such as LeBlon, Goethe, M.E. Chevreul, and Walter Sargent.

From a perspective of physics we can indicate the color of the shortest wavelength to be more energetic than that of the longest wavelength with the slowest vibratory rate of visible color. Considering our two polarities of color and the two polarities of active and passive in nature, we can see the active force in the fastest vibratory color ray and the passive force in the longest wavelength color ray. In the triad of color paints, blue is considered the active force, closest to the vibratory of violet in our spectral range. (The two color rays of the shortest wavelengths, indigo and violet, are considered by many as transcendental rays or rays irrelevant to the functioning of present humanity's level of evolution.). Red is seen as a passive force, denser and, thus, more material. Red and blue by themselves in painted color combinations would be rather limited. A third factor, the intermediary component, is needed and discovered in yellow. As we become more involved in the true significance and psychological effects of the various colors of the spectrum, we shall learn blue to be the more spiritual aspect of man, red the most physical, and yellow correspondent to the mind of man.

In the ancient teachings a primary triad to all life has been depicted in: WILL — ACTIVITY — LOVE. Through Will we have the motivating power of the spirit. This power of creating is seen in the Christian Trinity as God the Father. Geared more toward the spiritual aspect of man, the color blue corresponds to this power of spirit in man. The Will can be made manifest only through Activity, represented by the color red and in Christianity by the power of activity and disintegration of the Holy Ghost. The mediating power between the force of the Will and the form of the Activity is found in the power of Love. For Love provides an understanding gained from the necessity to balance off physical experience and the intuition of the spiritual will. Through this interaction of these two forces comes wisdom. In the Christian Trinity this power is seen in Christ the Son, symbolizing the united functioning of both the Will of the spirit and the Activity of the physical form. Through this interaction the Christ epitomized perfect Love, as when he stated in Luke 23:34, "Father, forgive them; for they know not what they do."

Not only has Christian theology been aware of the triad of the process of life. Many other systems have expressed the same principles in different terms. Hinduism emphasizes the supreme triad of Brahma, Vishnu, and Shiva, which represent the three paths or methods of release from transmigration (reincarnation). These paths in Hinduism are known as the path of knowledge, the path of selfless action, and the path of devotion to God. In China these three functions were explained in the concept of Yang (positive, active, masculine) and Yin (negative, passive, feminine), both of which were regulated by the Tao. The medieval alchemists saw all of life as varying combinations of salt, sulphur, and mercury.

Three symbolizes the dynamics of the process of life. Without a third factor between the two polarities of nature there could be no interaction, no joining together, no balancing influence—no life. When we speak of life, we arrive at our final number for present consideration: the number seven. For life on this physical plane is represented by the number seven. The number seven combines the three and the four. We have just seen the importance of the three in the dynamics of life process. In the four we have the geometrical representation of the square, indicating the solid foundation upon which material conditions are based. The four elements of astrology—fire, earth, air, water—are essential factors to the existence of life under these earthly conditions. In a sense, the three and four are comparable to the one and two, for in the three we have the force of dynamics and in the four we have the form of foundation. Both numbers give an indication of the alternation in the cycle of numbers between the polarities of positive-negative, odd-even, masculine-feminine. Although the four has similarities to the number two, in the four we move beyond mere duality in nature and through the interaction of the two forces (by means of the three) proceed to variety, multiplicity, and a foundation for continuing evolution.

Besides the geometrical significance of the number seven, we find the number seven repeatedly in our understanding of earth conditions. There are seven days of creation in the Book of Genesis in the Bible, and in the Revelation of Saint John the Divine we learn of "the seven Spirits of God sent forth into all the earth." (Revelation 5:6). These seven spirits are known as the seven Archangels of Christian theology and represent the seven creative spirits of differentiated energies, which are referred to as the Rishis or Sons of Wisdom in Eastern teachings. These seven creative spirits are seen in spiritual teachings as the formative forces in man's evolutionary path. According to spiritual teachings, there are seven rays of development open to the individual entity by which he can learn the lessons necessary for continued evolution toward the light of perfected awareness. These seven rays of development include:

1. will—by means of the will all things are set into motion. Based on an instinctual understanding of one's function in life, the individual focused on the ray of will has a determination and persistence to achieve his purpose no matter what obstacles arise.

2. love—with the love ray accentuated the individual entity gives totally of himself. There is no holding back but rather a total sharing of oneself with others and with no thought of a reward involved. This idea of love conflicts with the present mode of love, where desire assumes the form of love and dictates possession of the loved one.

3. activity—the individual concentrated upon this ray of development is concerned with organization, order, and the carrying out of the details of any situation. The intellect is attuned to the development of the reasoning faculties.

4. harmony—by means of harmony, there is an understanding of the balancing of life. Beauty,

gracefulness, and the esthetic come to the fore in the individual on the harmonic ray.

5. science—for those on the scientific ray life becomes an appreciation of the mathematical formula behind everything. Exactitude and total immersion in the study of any object are represented in these individuals. These people constantly search for knowledge and understanding.

6. devotion—this ray focuses upon faith and intuition. People with this ray emphasized in their beings are seen as the true patriots, supporting the established foundations of the culture.

7. ceremonial—this ray gives an understanding of the universal order. Recognizing the fact that all life has an order and structure for its proper functioning, people on this ray are seen as great orderers in their own lives.

Seven comes up repeatedly in the context of existence. In Rosicrucian teachings we discover seven basic principles associated with the cosmos. Although we have dealt with some of these principles in earlier pages, let us succinctly enumerate these principles as defined by Magus Incognito in the exposition, *The Secret Doctrines of the Rosicrucians*. These seven cosmic principles are:

1. Correspondence—alluded to in the adage, "As above, so below; as below, so above." This principle indicates the correspondence between tangible form of matter and the energy contained within the form. Correspondence recognizes the innumerable parallels between man (the microcosm) and his universal environment (the macrocosm).

2. Law and Order—just as everything in life is relative, this principle underlies the sequential phases to any ordering process. In any action

we set into process certain causes that lead us through a sequential process to arrive eventually at our considered effect.

3. Vibration—this principle emphasizes all life as energy and energy patterns as manifesting in various shapes or forms. We have seen this fact operative in our differentiated color rays, where the vibratory rates of the wavelengths of light rays determine the color of the ray.

4. Rhythm—this principle returns to our idea of alternation between the dual poles of nature. Life phenomena pulsate through the rhythmic process of ebb and flow, waxing and waning, output and input. Through rhythmic living we can attain health and well-being in our own lives.

5. Cycles—not only does life alternate rhythmically between the poles, but this principle indicates a continual progression in this alternation. Recall our symbol of infinity (∞). To incorporate more than one rhythmic alternation, we would not have the singular lemniscate, but rather something akin to the ribbon candy that fascinated us as children. Our lemniscate would become a series of such figures, spiraling both upwards and downwards.

6. Polarity—this principle enumerates the duality in life. Within every living thing is contained its opposite. Within form is the containment of energy. Within energy is the latency of manifestation in form. By becoming conscious of the polarities of nature, man has the opportunity to heed the Buddha's advice of following the middle way where man seeks the center as the point of equilibrium.

7. Sex—recognizing the two polarities of masculine-feminine in nature, this principle indicates the need for our third factor, our mediating

58

factor, our catalyst for union. From generation through sex comes creation, and the dynamics of life process are set into motion.

We have mentioned the continuing spiral of evolution and the idea of our ribbon-candy existence in the cycles and alternations of duality. Again we interpose the number seven. For in the process of earthly conditions we discover a phenomenon we call the Law of Octaves. The Law of Octaves indicates a sevenfold cycle prior to the beginning of the next cycle. We can see this law in the classification of chemical elements by the Periodic Table, devised by Dmitri Mendelejeff. We note it in the diatonic music scale. We observe it in astrology as indicative of the planetary energies. Until recently (1781) in astrological science there were seven differentiated energies symbolized by the planets. Revered by the ancients in their deep understanding of life process, these seven planets are: sun, moon, Mercury, Venus, Mars, Jupiter, Saturn. Each of these seven planets (for in astrological jargon we term the sun and moon as planets, although we recognize they are not planets as such) represents a different energy essential to the life conditions on our planet. Since 1781, however, we have discovered three more planets—Uranus, Neptune, Pluto—and astrologers have debated the existence of at least two others. In astrology there is an understanding of the Law of Octaves. While each planet represents differentiated energies, the three modern planets are considered as similar energies of three of the ancient planets but of a higher octave.

As we discussed Newton's color spectrum in our last chapter, we can understand the seven-tiered existence through the refraction of white light. We have indicated the difference of color by means of the difference in wavelengths of each color ray, whether they be the longer wavelengths toward the red end of the spectrum or the shorter wavelengths toward the violet end of the spectrum. We shall soon discover colors to be not

59

only physically differentiated energies but also energies affecting our psyches in different ways. Each of us is an individual. Each of us is a unique entity. Each of us responds to the colors of the spectrum in a different way. Some of us like colors that others find unbearable. Later in the book we shall discuss a means of self-analysis through the use of color. The self-analysis technique explained is intended to allow each of us to increase our awareness of the differentiating energies and the psychological effects of the various colors. By increased consciousness of the energies around us we can guide our lives toward greater tranquillity, harmony, and beauty.

But before we involve ourselves in our psyches, let us look at the principles of seven as they relate to our physical bodies. The ancient teachings have long considered man to be composed of both the triangle and the square. The head, chest and abdomen make up the triad of man, while the two arms and the two legs are the square of man. Noteworthy in this representation is our recognition of the positive force of three and the negative form of four. Thus, man has within himself both the positive and negative of nature. In the cranial, thoracic, and abdominal cavities are the essentials to the dynamics of life process within our bodies, and in our arms and legs are the material form of our movement.

Although man is presently aware of five sense organs inherent in his species, man in actual fact has seven senses. The five senses we are aware of are our faculties of touch, taste, smell, sight, and hearing. The sixth sense which all of man will eventually develop is an attribute of the negative, receptive, feminine pole of life. This sixth sense is more developed in women and facetiously named "woman's intuition." Of course, those who facetiously refer to this sixth sense as an abnormality of woman's character are often those totally involved in the outer-directed arc of existence. Lost to the balance in life, such people see the alternative pole as something opposed to them. Due to their own imbalance and lack of harmony, these people castigate the faculties of intuition and perception. In reality, however, intuition has been a saving grace to our culture. Similar to its development in women, master artists, scientists, and inventors have developed their faculties of intuition to serve as channels for inspiration and thereby create the forms necessary for their expression. This faculty of intuition or perception can be observed in the example of the Christ, who personifies a level of consciousness termed the Christos in the Gnosis. When the Christ walks upon water, we have allusion to the ability to rise above the waters of the emotions, to transcend the continual flux we live between despair and delight, to perceive clearly the reality of the life process. In the Spiritual teachings the Christos becomes a level toward which each one of us can aspire. As the Christ was born in the manger, so too are we born with the characteristics of animal passions. But as the Christ was able to remove himself from the stable of animal desires, so too can we ignite the spark of divinity within each one of us by our continual self-searching and constant self-development. By such a concentration we can attain a level of consciousness where we perceive reality without our transitory desires, whims, or opinions distorting the view. As the sense of intuition becomes more developed in humanity, so too will an ability to understand the reality of the life process and to communicate without tangible forms of communication.

This seventh sense is already coming to the fore. Similar to the advance of electronics beyond electricity with physical linkage no longer necessary for the transmission and reception of a message, so too will our forms of communication evolve to a level of thought transference. In contrast to our present forms of communication where thoughts are transferred to oral or written expression, man's ability to communicate is evolving to a point where he will communicate with others merely by the transmitting of thought-forms. Already each of us can see examples of thought transference in our daily lives. Most of us can probably recall experiences of thinking about someone and then unexpectedly receiving some tangible form of communication from that person. Or the times we have been with someone and blurted out an idea which the other person was thinking about. Although we pass off such incidents as coincidental, what is in actual fact occurring at such times is a form of thought transference. Like a transmitter we are unconsciously sending out certain messages, and the other person has unconsciously picked up the message and responded. Reqall our discussion of man's electrical body, and the way every living form is a container of energy with some of the energy emanating out from the form itself. Similar to our electrical body, our thoughts and feelings radiate out from us. Once we clear our minds of the interference produced by society's standards, by insecurities of self, and by other blockages to effective mental functioning, we will be able to develop our seventh sense of thought transference and grow toward a conscious understanding of our frequency transmission and registration.

In dealing with the electric body of man let us understand that there are certain points or vortices in this "body" by which energy is absorbed. Called the Chakras, these energy vortices are related to the endocrine glands and to locations along the spinal cord. Energy from the universal environment is drawn into the body. Like the prism's refraction of light into seven colors, the universal energy is refracted and sent to each chakra to energize the endocrine glands. These glands are the alchemists of the body, transmuting chemical elements into hormones to be carried through the blood stream. Parallel to the seven colors of the spectrum, each of these seven chakras has a different function in the body.

The Muladhara chakra is located at the base of the spine, in the coccygeal or gonad center. Through this chakra our bodies are supplied with physical energy. Related to the physical etheric plane of man's being, this chakra is affiliated with the color red.

The Svadhisthana chakra is located in the splenic center, in the small of the back. Related to the astral plane or the emotional nature of man, this chakra energizes both the physical and mental bodies, for it lies between the red ray of physical activity and the yellow ray of mental purpose. The Svadhisthana chakra corresponds to the color orange.

The Manipura chakra is located in the solar plexus center. Related to the lower mental plane of man's being, this chakra energizes man's lower mind—the objective, material realms of the mental faculties. Here we find the intellect, but an intellect attached to man's reasoning nature and, thus, the limits of his knowledge. The Manipura chakra serves as a filtering process, purifying the system of toxins in the digestive system, the adrenal glands, the pancreas, and the liver. This chakra corresponds to the color yellow.

The Anahata chakra is located at the cardiac plexus and affects both the heart and the blood pressure. Related to man's higher mind, this chakra affects the subjective, abstract realms of the mental faculties. More attuned to imagination than the lower mental plane, this chakra is also associated with emotions of a higher caliber than mere maudlin emotion. Here the emotions involved are empathy, understanding, and tenderness. Associated with the color green, this chakra is the balancing, harmonizing element in the body.

The Vishuddha chakra is located in the throat and associated with the thyroid gland. Based in the throat center, it influences man's ability to express himself through oral communication. As well, the initial thrust of the spiritual aspect of man, man's faith, is found here. This chakra corresponds to the color blue.

The Ajna chakra is located in the pineal gland, often depicted in spiritual illustrations as the third eye. Both this chakra, correspondent to the color indigo, and the following chakra, correspondent to the color violet, are considered transcendental chakras. In other words, these two chakras are not yet developed in the average man. Similar to the sixth and seventh sense in man, these chakras are considered as potentials rather than actualities. The Ajna chakra relates to man's intuitional faculties beyond the mere reasoning faculties. This potential faculty is akin to the inspiration received from intangible sources, the impressions or images that seem to come to us from out of nowhere. Through the proper functioning of this chakra, man begins to know. Although he cannot explain logically to non-believers, the man with his intuitive faculties developed begins to recognize the process of life and to appreciate the alternating phases of the process. Fears, inhibitions, and insecurities in his life start to fall away, for he becomes more perceptive.

The Sahasrara chakra, correspondent to the color violet, has been termed the thousand-petalled lotus. Located at the dome of the head and associated with the pituitary gland, this chakra relates to the spiritual element in man and approaches a functioning on a level similar to the Christos. No longer are there questions or answers but a state of total awareness. Similar to the violet color ray, this chakra represents the highest vibratory frequency of cosmic energy to be taken into man.

Through these seven chakras man absorbs into his body much of the universal energy needed to maintain the functioning of his organism. As the chakras are energy vortices, they are similar to any container of energy, and, thus, must reflect some of the energy outward. We again return to our electrical body of man, recognizing that the energy reflected outward from each chakra makes up the seven layers of the electrical body. The layer closest to the physical body relates to the Muladhara chakra in the coccygeal center and to the red color ray. The next layer is associated with the Svadhisthana chakra and the color orange, and so forth through the layers of the electrical body. Since the two chakras correspondent to the indigo and violet color rays are not developed in the average individual, most people have five layers to their electrical body. At some period man will claim his heritage to develop his sixth and seventh senses and will function with all seven chakras operating.

As such a state is in the future for most of us, let us return to the present and proceed to the psychological aspects of color. In this chapter we have seen the significance of numbers and the correlation of our colors to the phenomena of life process. We are now ready to understand the practical use of color and will undertake an investigation of the psychological effects of color. Later we will work with a combination of numerology and color as an aid to increased self-understanding. But on with the colors.

Chapter 4

The Primary Colors

Through our experience with color we derive our understanding of color. Although we may have begun to recognize the correlation between color rays and differing energy levels, our knowledge of color is still predominantly dependent upon our use of color in our wardrobes, furnishings, and environment. But how do we choose colors with which to surround ourselves? Our choices are usually based upon our whims, our likes, and our dislikes. Too often our preferences are unconscious choices instead of based on a true understanding of the energy differentials and their subsequent varying psychological effects on us. As each one of us is different, each of us will have different preferences in our choice of colors. If we were more aware of the significance of the different colors, we could employ the varying energies and functions of these colors in a more conscious manner and in a manner beneficial to our greater well-being.

Prior to our explanation of the meanings of the colors, let us test our own preferences. In order to do so, obtain for yourself fabrics of the seven colors of Newton's spectrum: red-orange-yellow-green-blue-indigo-violet. Place them before you and consider each one individually. How does each color affect you? Which of these colors do you like the most? Which do you like the least? With which of these colors do you surround yourself?

Select the colors in order of your preference. Once you have so arranged the colors, reflect again on these colors. See where they appear in your life, how they affect your life. As we have mentioned previously, color is energy and must affect us in varying ways in accordance with the differences of the energy level of each color ray. If we are oblivious to the effects of color, we could be surrounding ourselves with colors detrimental to our well-being. If we are not aware of the true significance and psychological effects of the various colors, how can we know the consequences that colors have upon our world?

Let us explore the colors then for their characteristic manner of expression. Not only will we indicate the basic qualities of the colors, but for our later purpose of self-analysis we will explain how people with each of these colors predominant in their being might act in their life situations. As true knowledge is a combination of our learning and our experiences, let each of us reflect upon the validity of the characteristics outlined. We should neither accept the ideas blindly nor reject such concepts offhand. Consider the characteristics of the colors and test their validity through your own experience. By so doing it is possible that you may gain several meaningful insights into the world of color which you can later incorporate in the conscious coloring of your own world.

RED

To consider our range of colors we will start at the red end of the spectrum. Having the longest wavelength of the color rays of the spectrum, the red ray is more related to the material realm of man than is the violet end of the spectrum where the vibrancy of energy is more associated with the spiritual aspect of man. Red corresponds to the Muladhara chakra, through which we draw the refraction of the universal energy to provide our bodies with physical energy. Therefore, it should not be surprising to learn that red is representative of physical energy. Red has a vitalizing effect on our bodies. Exciting and enlivening, it gets the adrenalin going. As a stimulant to both the physical body and the nervous system, red can be successfully employed for those times when we feel totally run down. Try it yourself sometime. When you feel exhausted and need more energy, concentrate on the color red. This focusing can be performed by wearing red, by eating red-colored food, or by the mere mental focusing on the color with an understanding of its significance.

In red we have the initiating cause. Red is the initiator, the creator, the pioneer. Red prefers to lead rather than to follow. If red were forced to follow the lead of others, the result could be frustration, anger, and a constant chomping at the bit. Red must be able to go its own way without restraint. Representing the initial phase of self-assertion, red needs avenues for expression. For red is the "I AM" function of being, the primal expression of the individuality, as in the first stream of life. The life process purpose of those with red heavily accentuated in their being is to individualize. They need to be their own masters, to stand on their own two feet, to assert their own selves.

Being an expansive energy, red overcomes inertia and depression. But red has an insatiable ambition and without proper restraints or considered judgment its action can lead to an outward drive having no limits either in purpose or in means. Red's energy is of an unrefined nature. While there is great physical strength, it is of a brute force.

Studies have found that red is preferred by those who might be classified as extroverts in contrast to introverts. Remember that red is a concentration upon the external experiences of life with no holds barred. Life is lived to its fullest. Reflection upon life experiences must await the other colors, for red's purpose is to experience, to express, to be. As red is an advancing color, it produces movement and activity. We have mentioned in previous pages the fact that a total focus on red could lead to inflammatory or feverish conditions. This is true not only as it affects the physical body but also in regard to the mental-emotional being as well. Without the necessary constructive outlets to allow for self-expression the energy called forth can lead to restlessness and nervous tension debilitating to the body. Energy can be scattered and aims lost, as the life becomes a whirlwind of activity without center, without direction, solely an attempt to "get while the getting is good" without any recognition of what one is getting.

Being at one extreme of the spectrum, red's primary problem is the tendency to go to extremes in behavior. Balance is hard to achieve. Too often red sees nothing but the objectives. Details and the means to achieve its purpose are lost to the vision of its anticipated results. At one extreme, red's ambition can lead to domination, aggression, and the shedding of blood to attain its aims. At the other extreme, when confronted by an obstacle and unable to cope with the challenge, red may decide to withdraw, to retreat from action, to become indolent and totally dependent upon others for its life support.

With an emphasis upon self-expression, red is often related to procreation, generation, and sexual intercourse. Being an emotional color, it has an incredible depth of passion to it. Typical of the red temperament, this passion also ranges between the extremes of an ardent love nature to an aggressive desire nature. When manifesting as the love nature, red can move its objectives forward courageously, without fear or concern for its own safety. The intensity of love in red can incite it to fight for a principle with fortitude, no matter how strong the opposition. The expansive nature of red's love leads to a generosity that will sacrifice itself should the need arise. On the other hand, the aggressive desire nature of red can lead to a possessiveness that totally consumes the object of the love. Everything must bow to the power of the desire nature. Neglecting constructive channels for expression, the energy then focuses upon an outward thrust of domination and total self-interest. Such passion can result in a cruelty and tyranny that submit to none but seek to conquer all.

ORANGE

In orange we have a balancing color, for orange is considered a secondary color, partaking of both red and yellow. As orange lies between red and yellow, it has an effect on both the physical well-being (red) and the intellect (yellow). Similar to the red ray, it has an enlivening effect and provides energy to cope with life's situations. Stimulating to the nerves, orange lends itself to a buoyancy of spirit. This exuberance of life is emotionally colored, for the intellect of yellow has not become strong enough in orange to limit this joy within reasonable bounds. Therefore, orange can lead to an extreme state of self-indulgence. Dissimilar to the uncontrolled ricochet of extremes possible in the red focus, orange does have some reason behind its action, due to the initial seeping of yellow's intellect into the character of the orange color. Orange brings tolerance to action and greater understanding to its use of energy. Just as orange serves as the bridge between the red and yellow color rays, so too does orange allow for greater balance in activity.

Being a cheerful, warm color, orange can be used to remove fears or inhibitions from living. It sparks a mental enlightenment and a sense of freedom from restrictions. For those who feel mentally catatonic, unable to handle life's opportunities and challenges, orange might prove an effective elixir. Aiding the expansion of the mind, orange allows new ideas entry into the realm of mental consideration. Not only can orange heal the body physically, but it provides a certain understanding of both the need and the methods to keep the body functioning at an optimum level. Orange serves the function of assimilation of mental concepts. Through orange man can transform his nature from the purely physical, which is virtually equivalent to the animal level of operating on mere instinct, to a higher plateau where he can begin to use his reasoning faculties to influence his actions.

Orange functions as a peacemaker, having as its purpose the attainment of harmony, relatedness, and association. In the combination of the power of the red color ray and the intellect of the yellow color ray, orange has the energy and interest to delve into situations, dissect the components, and then integrate the parts into a balanced whole. The power of orange is in its ability to bring together information, people, or incidents into cooperative unity. As the blending process is all-important to it, orange has a tendency to see both sides to any question. Tactful in expression, orange can make an art out of its talent of persuasion. Rhythm and timing are usually pronounced in orange. As well, there is a sense of the esthetic, a hunger for peace, and an appreciation of form. As a result, orange often presents a suavity, grace, and charm in its bearing.

Since balance is but a point of equilibrium in constant flux, orange finds times when the balance within itself is lacking. At these moments orange tends to go to the extremes of its neighbors in the color spectrum, red and yellow. Polarized toward the red ray, orange can burst forth with incredible anger, haste, and recklessness that shows no reasoning whatsoever. At the other extreme, orange's move toward the yellow ray leads it to use the intellect as a means to flail out at restrictions. It then becomes impossible to reason with the orange, for its likes and dislikes become a fortified castle that even patient, considered judgment cannot penetrate.

The determination in orange can become exacting in its demands for the perfecting of balance both in itself and in others. Consideration of and cooperation with others is lost to a hyper-criticism. Launched against itself, this criticism can make the orange timid, self-deprecating, and fearful of failure. Indecision arises and, in consequence, a dependence upon others.

Although orange wants to associate with others, it is essential for the orange to stress self-confidence. In seeking to please others it should not lose its ability to be itself. For the orange does have the tendency to be overconscientious and overly considerate. What others say and do affects the orange greatly, for it is impressionable both to the people in its environment and to its surroundings. This sensitivity of the orange can allow its imagination to run riot with forebodings that have no basis in reality. In action and in thought the orange should always remember the key word: balance.

YELLOW

At yellow we arrive at the level of the intellect. By means of the intellect man separates himself from the animal nature inherent in his species. Reason gives man the capability to understand. No longer need he rely upon instinct to survive. With yellow man has the opportunity to think and acquires greater self-control than with the energies of the two previously discussed colors of orange and red. An inspiring color, yellow awakens and stimulates the mental faculties. Absorbed in the world of ideas, yellow has a keen mind with sharp mental discernment that borders on the prophetic in its sensing of impressions.

Affecting the nervous system, yellow can relax those who are perplexed by life's lessons and find themselves down in the doldrums. Negative feelings are countered by yellow, for the light, warm color radiates optimism and joyousness.

With its emphasis upon the mind rather than the body, yellow can neglect the physical body and the more practical aspects of life. Yellow often creates castles in the air, for it tends to flights of fancy and dreams of grandeur. Reality is considered painful. Yellow prefers to follow the yellow brick road of imagination and fantasy. It constantly presses forward toward the future, toward the unknown, leaving the present lost in its visions. As there is much diversity and originality to the yellow, it can develop any one of its many talents to a level of proficiency. But where the problem can arise with the yellow temperament is in this quality of diversity.

For diversity is all-important to the yellow. Variety, spontaneity, and a constant change that almost reaches the point of change for change's sake, are integral parts to its makeup. Although there is much activity to the yellow, the activity comes in compulsive spurts. Yellow tends to lack concentration and has difficulty seeing any one thing through to completion. Lying behind yellow's path is a view of discarded, unfinished tasks or projects. Scattering its energies and spreading itself thin, yellow has something of a superficiality to it.

Hand in hand with the need for variety is the essential of freedom. If yellow does not have the freedom to pursue its activities according to its own mode of action, it spends its energies whining, criticizing, and gossiping. Whenever the sunshine of its life is clouded over, it can exhibit such negative qualities as deceit, envy, selfishness, and sensation-seeking.

Among yellow's functions is the expression of self. Unlike red this expression is not the primal scream of self-assertion, but rather a more refined expression of creativity. With the intellect attuned, yellow revels in learning and in the discussing of what it has learned. Yellow has a gift for words and dresses them imagina-

74

tively with a zest of living. An inspiring, expansive color, it takes every opportunity to communicate with others. For much of yellow's enjoyment in life is to spread sunshine. At times impatience can lead to intolerance, which clouds the pleasing, charming personality of the yellow. This attitude can result in strife and selfishness. The yellow should try to restrain a self-centeredness and a dogmatism regarding the validity of its own opinions.

Capable of deep affection, yellow is desirous of admiration and popularity. The yellow is often surrounded by friends, like moths fluttering around a bright light, for the sparkling personality of the yellow attracts flocks of admirers. As sharing the wells of its thought springs vitalizes the yellow, it should seek a wide circle of friends and acquaintances as avenues for greater self-expression. Pleasure is a great part of the yellow's life, and it should do all it can to give out as much as it receives. For in the giving the yellow will receive several-fold in return.

GREEN

In green we see the color of nature. As nature maintains a degree of balance between its multitude of forces amidst continual change, so too does the color green represent balance. For green lies midway between the red end and the violet end of the color spectrum. It is here that a balance is struck between man's material aspect of being and the spiritual aspect of man. There is harmony, peace, and serenity achieved in the color green.

Relaxing and refreshing, green is a pleasing color. As strain is alleviated through balancing, green can soothe tension in the muscles and nerves. Green does not inflame or aggravate but quiets and refreshens. From its neighbors on the color spectrum green shares in the happiness of yellow and the tranquillity of blue. In green we have the representation of life. With the

75

advent of spring, green buds on trees and shrubs burst forth to offer each of us the hope of the season's renewal, growth, life. The growth of green indicates the maturing of both man's physical body and his mind. With green the body contains the physical energy in a poised manner, and the mind progresses from initial mental ramblings to a practical application of its mental faculties.

Green begins to understand that life has a purpose and seeks to create purpose for its own expression. Green tends to be highly determined, efficient, and conscientious in its endeavors. Patient and attentive to detail, green is the one who often completes the tasks others leave unfinished. From its innate sense of balance green recognizes the importance of proportions and precision. Green enforces an order and system of regularity in its life. It should be wary that routine does not narrow its vision and lead to a paralyzing rigidity. Dependable, serious, and ambitious to achieve concrete results, green constructs and supports the solid foundations for life. Ideas are brought down to earth and given shape in forms which are arranged in a harmonious relationship one with another.

From its organization of life into systems and forms, green creates a sense of security for itself. Tradition-bound, green has difficulty at times with anything avant-garde or new. Relying on the equilibrium of the status quo, green fears and even disdains change. Permanency is sought, but nothing is as permanent as change. A desire for security can lead green on a quest for power over others. Although green can prove an able director and manager of life's practical affairs, too often there is an overbearing attitude which conveys not only the insecure need to impress others but the desire to have its own way, no matter what. Instead of attempting to adapt and reconcile different viewpoints, green then interprets balance as control over its surroundings, whether life situations or people.

At its worst, green can exhibit dogmatism, envy, and

cruelty. Nothing is allowed to stop green's endeavors. If green feels the need to destroy the forms of others in order to construct its own forms, then green will do so without remorse. For green finds it essential to construct life according to its own dictates. When life is disturbed by unsettled conditions, thereby threatening its security, green can become discontent and restless to the point of violent action.

Green should try to cultivate a broader vision, for its lack of imagination and its narrowness allow a clinging to convention and established modes. Within the green is the desire to nourish, to help others to grow and develop. Although green can serve as the architect and builder of institutions for the benefit of all, when it becomes overly self-interested, its fine qualities are lost to a sordid state of being. Green should constantly take the time to reflect upon its qualities of color: the continual source of hope for renewal, the capability to construct forms to serve a definite purpose, and the efficiency of order to complete tasks yet unfinished. Through such focusing, green can achieve its true balance.

BLUE

In blue we move away from the mere physical and toward the spiritual aspects of life. As seen in the sky and in the oceans, blue represents an infinitude to being. In blue we have the feeling of depth. The temporal is lost to the comfort of the eternal. Spiritual contentment and joy are expressed by blue. With blue's nascent link to the endless process of life, truth becomes more pronounced—not the truth as interpreted by man's ignorance but the truth of objective reality.

A peaceful, relaxing color, blue can soothe distraught nerves or the anquish of mental strain. It has a pacifying effect on the nervous system and creates greater tranquillity in its surroundings. Blue settles and makes secure. Despite this calming effect, blue also has something of a stimulating effect. The stimulation of blue is not of a physical force but rather a spiritual force of upliftment. Recall blue's effect in our own lives when we have taken the opportunity to detach ourselves from our mental ramblings and fearful rumblings to look quietly at the blue of the sky, at the continual movement in our oceans, at the ripplings across a lake or the rush of water downstream. At such times, hasn't a feeling of tranquillity filled each one of us? Our fears have been quieted, for what have we to fear? In the depths of the nature of blue we can see the depths of continual process. Our superficialities give way to faith, to an innate belief in the truth of reality. Blue instills in us moments of introspective awareness when we can touch base with our inner being and calm ourselves from the external agonies of our own creation.

Blue offers a quietude of spirit, a tranquillity of bearing, an inner peace. Built upon its devotion to realize its connection with the universal environment, blue is stable and dependable. Although soothing in nature, blue does not lie idle, for it aspires to seek the substance and truth to every reality. As if in becoming one with each experience, blue sees the chance to expand and evolve further in its own self-understanding and development. Blue lives life to the fullest and often has many irons in the fire. Incredibly versatile, blue can deal with any number of situations at one time.

Searching life experiences for their underlying reality, blue involves itself in concerns beyond the mere practicalities of earthly existence. Blue seeks truth in everything. Without the need for a formalized education, blue seems to understand innately various aspects of life. The insecurity of the ego falls away from the blue, for within its being is a trust and faith in its own essential security. It desires to influence others not out of self-conceit but to project the good things in life to all.

There is something of the unconventional in blue. From the recognition that man is not totally restricted to the corporeality of his form, blue strives for freedom in all it does. Blue begins to break away from the routines and standards of society which could prove limiting to its search for adventure. Motivated by a natural curiosity to corroborate its innate understanding of life with knowledge of experience, blue takes an active part in the world. It recognizes in every experience a lesson to be learned. Its inherent security allows blue to adapt to changing conditions. Change, progress, and the unknown animate the blue.

If its faith is shaken, blue can respond to the negative attributes of its color. Either it becomes lazy, apathetic, and indulgent of its own whims, or it becomes impatient, rash, and totally irresponsible. The versatility of interests can lead to a lack of constancy, as blue seeks the thrills of life. It maintains its freedom but accomplishes nothing. Blue's faith turns to superstition, as the imagination runs riot. Dissatisfied and critical of everything, blue no longer trusts to its essential self but scurries around to accumulate physical goods for its security.

Manifestation of the negative aspects of blue is unfortunate, for within blue is much love and beauty. If properly applied, its devotion and aspirations can lead to a public life where blue can inspire and uplift those struggling in the storms of continual process. Through its sharp mind, observant qualities, and gift of expression, blue can communicate its understanding of life's process and assist others to live their lives more happily.

INDIGO

With indigo spiritual understanding continues to unfold. No longer is this understanding based solely upon faith and devotion as with blue but rather becomes more attuned to the reality of living. With a developed intuition, indigo integrates this process of understanding within itself. However, as we mentioned in our discussion of man's sense faculties and the seven chakras, recognize that man's use of the energy frequency of indigo is primarily at a latent level at present. While the five previously discussed colors are used extensively in our furnishings, our wardrobes, and our life accoutrements, indigo and violet are not used as extensively.

Indigo helps relieve the inner energies of man from its fears, frustrations, and inhibitions. Similar to blue's function of uplifting the mind, indigo offers the opportunity to perceive more clearly the reality of the life process. The consciousness is focused upon worlds beyond the physical manifestation. Man's dual nature of the spiritual and the material becomes more integrated and better understood. A sense of unity within man is established. No longer are the energies concentrated solely on the external, outer-directed arc of existence. Rather, indigo affords a greater receptivity in order to allow impressions a fertile ground for increased perception.

Indigo's understanding of the life process gives it the function to serve mankind. Indigo can be the philosopher and adjuster of life's problems and situations. Given an intuitive understanding of the life process, indigo is asked to transmit its understanding to others. As a result, indigo is often involved in the idealistic and artistic, seeking to create the beauty of life among the sordid conditions man has constructed for his living. Indigo seeks justice and fairness in all dealings. It is the indigo who is called upon to adapt situations to a harmonious unity. For within the indigo is tolerance and a recognition of the mire in which others allow themselves to live. The discrepancy between its dreams and mankind's reality serves to spur indigo on to greater works and accomplishment in behalf of all. While indigo may be accused of being unrealistic by those who do not have the perception of indigo, indigo lives on a level where it senses the beauty in all of life. Indigo must express this beauty, and from its expression mankind gains comfort and happiness. Love is important to indigo, for without love it feels there is no purpose to

80

life and no appreciation of the beauty of the process of life. Thus, indigo is often associated with a home, a family, and children. Translated further outward, indigo seeks love in all its relationships. Everything it says, everything it does, expresses the love deep within the indigo. This love can be felt by others who seek comfort and help from the indigo. Its time and its home become a refuge for all those torn or battered by life's alternating processes of lessons and opportunities. Yet despite the many calls made upon indigo, it asks to serve others in whatever way it can. No promise is left unfulfilled by indigo. If something awaits doing, the indigo will do it, for it has the courage and determination to pursue its purpose. Indigo is noble and compassionate. When manifesting the positive arc of its existence, it becomes a pillar of the community of man. As indigo can be used to free us of our inhibitions, so too does it seek to broaden the horizons of our mind, to communicate the dual aspects of life, to make clearer for each one of us the process of reality. Thanks to indigo, reforms are carried out at all levels of being.

As each color can manifest its energies in positive or negative ways, indigo too has negative attributes. Instead of serving as the universal comforter, indigo can decide to withdraw from the battle and live its life alone. Removing itself from the turbulence of the life process, indigo refuses any degree of responsibility. It tries then to be an island unto itself. The beauty of life it perceives becomes locked within. Blockages to free expression lead to a paralytic state of mind, resulting in a scattering of mental energies, forgetfulness, and fixed opinions and set ways. Its outlook changes from one of love to one of dogmatism, austerity, and a demand for approval and recognition from others. It becomes cynical, intolerant, inconsiderate. Its innate desire to serve inverts to its becoming an interfering busybody, not only unable to help others but unable to help itself. But the indigo temperament can control these energies. By proper direction of its energies, indigo can be of selfless service to others. This is its true purpose, for indigo has been given vast resources and must share its perception of life's beauty with others.

VIOLET

From the devotion of blue and the intuition of indigo, our color spectrum evolves to the level of violet, where the highest element in man's nature is represented. In violet there is a progression beyond blue's faith in the spiritual and indigo's intuitive perception of reality. Violet strives to consciously learn the reality of the life process. Violet sees the primal forces behind the appearance of established situations. Nothing is accepted at face value, for violet probes the depths of any situation to discover the reason why. Violet is motivated by a need to link consciously the known with the unknown. As knowledge is its purpose, violet is tireless in its pursuit to delve into the soul of any condition. It has an inspired mind and can understand the deeper facts of life's process. It searches the hidden, the obscure, the occult. For being at the end of the spiritually oriented side of the spectrum, violet is fascinated by its dreams, visions, inspirations.

Similar to the other cooling colors of blue and indigo, violet is beneficial for frayed nerves. Nervous strain is a result of imbalance and an inability to understand the phases in the process of living. With blue, indigo, and violet, the spiritual aspect of man is augmented, which leads to greater faith, perception, and conscious awareness of man's purpose in being. Thus, there is something calming in these colors to alleviate neuroses.

Just as violet completes one octave of the color spectrum, so too does violet seek perfection in life. But this concept of perfection should be read in terms of the transmutation about which the medieval alchemists spoke. For violet asks of man to search deep within himself and eventually transmute his desire nature by which the evolution of mankind is held back. Through such intensive investigation violet offers inspiration into the true meaning of life and the relative perfection of everything that partakes of life. Violet serves as a light-bearer, bringing mankind gifts of inspiration in the form of masterpiece works of art, thought, achievement. Violet strives for the ideal and willingly sacrifices itself to attain it.

Born with the essential security of its inner self, violet has a poise and refinement to its character. In search of the best in everything, violet often creates a tranquil and inspiring environment for itself. Violet is sensitive to the vibrations of others and of its surroundings. Although it is often considered a loner, violet needs time to be alone in order to meditate and absorb the insight of its studies, observations, and inspirations. It is necessary for violet to reflect upon experience and gain the composure of solitude, for violet is involved in the conscious linking between the physical and the super-physical, between the objective and the subjective.

Its emphasis upon the non-physical can sometimes lead violet to create enchanted worlds in which to live. Wish fulfillment then takes the place of action and effort. At such times, it devises a magical kingdom for its life, but a kingdom devoid of reality. For being at the extreme of one side of the spectrum, there is the tendency to separate from physical reality and to live its life in dreams of perfection. Excessive spirituality can lead to nebulousness and an inability to differentiate. While ecstatic in its dream world, violet senses a despair when reality all too suddenly confronts it. Violet then seeks escape into fantasy.

Violet is not an especially good mixer in public. Although there is much passion within the violet, it often has difficulty expressing itself with a sense of ease. Its reserved, discriminating nature can put people off. While it has the ability to charm and delight others, it is often unwilling to make the effort to do so. Living in a fantasy world, violet can devise all sorts of rules and roles for others to conform to. It can become proud, lost in its own self-esteem, and arrogant to the point of dominating any who dare enter its world. Violet can maintain its distance from others, which is unfortunate, for its inherent nature is one of kindness, gentility, and helpfulness. Although violet is capable of accomplishments respected by others, its emphasis upon its own individuality can undermine its efforts. With its inspired wit, keen perception, and striving for perfection, violet can be a leader and teacher to those who seek an understanding of the truth to the life process. At its best, violet can express the love and wisdom of life for others to understand. If it will transmute the base qualities of its desire nature into selfless service to others, violet can shed the light on truth and relative perfection.

As we will be dealing with the synthesis of color and the science of numbers in our technique for color self-analysis, the two initial colors of the next octave of the color spectrum have been included in our consideration of the characteristics of color. Although with violet we have completed our consideration of the seven colors that compose Newton's color spectrum, our range of numbers runs from 1 to 9. In the last chapter we mentioned the cycle of seven as the epitome of life under earthly conditions, for it combines the three of the dynamics of process with the four of the material foundation. While this pattern is valid, there is also a ninefold cycle which allows for the threefold process to occur fully within each phase of its beginning, middle, and end cycle. Thus, within the beginning phase of the process we have a threefold process of beginning-middle-end, within the middle phase we have the same threefold process, and likewise with the end phase of our larger cycle of process.

As we have talked of the Law of Octaves, we can understand that when a cycle is completed, the process does not end. Rather, the cycle starts again, but at a different level. Similar to the structure of a child's slinky toy, the life process is a continual spiraling of experience and cycles. The same is true of the color spectrum. When we reach the violet color at the more vibratory end of the spectrum, our colors do not end but progress again through the basic shades of the original seven colors. This next color cycle, however, is of a more ethereal nature and great vibratory rate.

Devoted to the art of color in his painting, Sir Winston Churchill implied this concept of octave ranges when he stated:

"I cannot pretend to be impartial about color. I rejoice with the brilliant ones and am genuinely sorry for the poor browns. When I get to heaven, I mean to spend the first million years in painting and so get to the bottom of the subject. But I shall require a still gayer palette than I get here below. I expect orange and vermillion will be the darkest, dullest colors upon it and beyond them there will be a whole range of wonderful new colors which will delight the celestial eye."

When we reach our eighth color, we arrive at the tone of red. But as with the beginning of every cycle in life, we do not start at the same point as the beginning of the previous cycle. No, that is an impossibility. After all, in our world of relativity we can recognize that the space-time coordinates are totally different. Recall the analogy Heraclitus used to our lives as rivers. Every change progression in time inherently causes a change in the spatial coordinates involved. But the space-time coordinate change is not the only change involved in our progression of color. Rather, we are dealing with a higher frequency, a more rapid wavelength, as we progress to the higher octave of Newton's color spectrum.

Therefore, while our eighth color will partake of much of the energy of red, it will be far more ethereal than red, in a sense far more evolved. To give a label to this color correspondent with its reality would be to

85

rigidify it to our present terms and concepts. Suffice it to say that our eighth color is of a higher octave of red and in its daily use we might relate it to our presently known shades of pink or rose.

HIGHER OCTAVE OF RED: ROSE, PINK

As we are dealing with the higher octave of red, this eighth color partakes of much of the energy of red. Rose also lies beyond the violet end of the spectrum and has in it a greater understanding of the life process. The eighth color manifests not solely as brute force or physical energy, but as a driving force directed along disciplined lines. The awareness of the life process combines with physical energy and leads rose to turning visions into realities. The purpose of this color is to harmoniously blend the infinitude of spiritual understanding with the finite of physical manifestation. Rose is able to bring the ethereal and spiritual into physical form. Yet it harbors few illusions, for it has gone through the entire octave to reach this level and understands the life conditions under which it must work.

The higher octave of red functions as a guide for mankind. On the positive arc this color can control its own moods and opinions and work in cooperation with others for the benefit of all. Understanding human psychology, rose is able to appreciate the emotions of others and works with the abilities of each individual to bring out optimum potential. Rose can judge impartially, can arbitrate between factions, and can direct the construction of the dreams of others. As an administrator, it works without prejudice but with a vast storehouse of knowledge. While growth and progress are important to rose, its ability to balance countervailing forces leads to acceptance and respect from its co-workers.

The blending of physical drive and spiritual knowledge motivates rose to accomplishment, and the accomplishments found most satisfying are those which benefit humanity. For in its understanding of the life process, rose recognizes the gestalt, the unity, the totality of all the components of existence. The rose is often involved in large-scale operations. It has the breadth of vision to see all the factors in a situation and to synthesize these factors into a working relationship to arrive at its goal. Aware that a prerequisite for spiritual development is to seek excellence in all that it does, rose seeks material perfection in its endeavors.

Although there are times when rose may seem exacting and demanding of others, on a positive arc rose will rarely spare itself. It expects only as much from others as it is willing to do itself. Yet the driving force and competence of rose is indefatigable. As if fulfillment of this internal driving force results from exertion and accomplishment, rose needs to achieve. Self-reliant and dependable, failure to the rose is a figment of other people's imaginations. While it may use people to attain the goal it envisions, the rose will constantly strive to assist others in perfecting their own expression. The rose never slackens but gives its all to attain its purposes.

While the rose may seem unemotional and demanding, much of its driving force comes from the prodding of its deep compassion for its fellow man. Its purpose is to help others. Its efforts are not self-aggrandizement as much as for the betterment of conditions for all mankind. The rose can display a loving affection and friendliness. Yet this lovingness and affection often have to take a back burner, for rose's life is filled by its desire to attain, to achieve, to realize in form the dreams of the world. Therefore, it is often difficult to get close to the rose. Pleasant, friendly get-togethers are fine for others but are too often considered an indulgence by rose. Such an attitude can lead to an isolation and loneliness for rose.

As with all colors, there are negative attributes to rose. Similar to red, rose can be bullying or overbearing in trying to achieve its purpose. The desire to serve humanity can become lost to a totally physical functioning, whereby spiritual understanding is forgotten. The need for security then becomes paramount, which rose seeks to find in the ability to control, to dominate, to command. Rose can become impatient and intolerant with others. With the material aspects emphasized, rose becomes lost in the mire of exploitation and accumulation. It strains to attain and loses balance. It becomes overactive and tense and debilitates the body. On a negative arc rose demands recognition and deceives others to gain power for itself. Such attitudes are unfortunate, for rose's true purpose is to administer, guide, and control others not from a vengeful, authoritarian stance but with loving kindness and a sharing of both its understandings and abilities.

HIGHER OCTAVE OF ORANGE: GOLD

With our ninth color we arrive at the higher octave of orange. As nine completes the cycle of process (as opposed to seven as the completion of life conditions on the earthly plane), so too does our ninth color, the higher octave of orange, symbolize a degree of perfection. Yet let us not forget that while one cycle is completed, an ending always signifies a new beginning. We have termed this color of the higher octave of orange as gold, for similar to the process described by the alchemists, our ninth color represents the completion of man's process of transmutation from the base metal of instinct and desire to the gold of the realization of the divine spark within him.

Correspondent to the energies of orange, gold is the light of joy and cheer. Hope, laughter, happiness emanate from gold. As orange balances the energies of physical force (red) and mental intellect (yellow), gold blends a driving energy with the wisdom of the ages. Gold serves to communicate cosmic love and truth to others. Gold is the sage, the wise counsellor. It has experienced all in life and now is called upon to translate its knowledge. Radiating vitality and warmth to nourish the souls and spirits of its brothers, gold has a strong influence upon the world. Its sympathy, understanding, and deep feeling for its fellow man win it respect and admiration.

Although gold may yearn for the respite of personal love, deep within itself is the recognition that its purpose is an impersonal mission of comforting and soothing others. Like the daily passage of the sun across the sky, gold symbolizes the world traveller who roams the four corners of the world to communicate its message of love, perfection, wisdom. Inspired, it can be a great artist, for the depth of emotion is unfathomable. On a positive arc gold transforms its base qualities, its passions, and instinctual nature into universal understanding and selfless service. Recognizing that life cannot be truly beautiful until all share in its beauty, gold interprets this beauty to others by casting rays of sunshine across the hearts of others. Love radiates from gold. While the rose may build concrete realities and structures out of the dreams and visions of others, it is gold who expresses the soul beauty in its words, thoughts, communications. Gold is the master teacher. For as a teacher gold is not pedantic, as violet may tend to be, but vitalizes all expression with its profound feeling of life, of warmth, of heart. Behind its expressions are spiritual force and magnetic appeal.

Gold is popular and well-liked, for its joy of living wins the admiration of all who enter its presence. While some may envy gold, gold is above petty desires. Eventually it wins converts to a joy of living. It does not enforce its message on others but merely seeks to share its thoughts with others with no threat of domination. Gold lives life with grace, cheer, spirituality. The intensity of its life comforts others. Where gold finds difficulty is in living up to its sense of perfection. If it feels that its ideals cannot be realized either by itself or by others, it tends to become discouraged.

Living too fully in the world of the abstract, it can detach itself from the realities others live.

When disappointed by the frustrations in life, gold may tend to dissipate its forces. The emotions become overly sensitized and the moods fluctuate between despair and delight. When the efforts of gold are not directed toward comforting and helping others, there can be a strong degree of self-indulgence. Gold then becomes changeable and lost in day-dreams. Gold may seek the easy way out, enjoying the pomp and circumstance of life yet offering nothing in return. On its negative arc, gold can manifest an incredible selfishness and a possessiveness of everything and everyone around it. If self-gratification becomes the purpose of gold, then misery must be its destiny. For an emphasis on taking rather than giving leads to a constant longing for satisfaction, a restless seeking for the missing factor to its completion. Fearful and indecisive, gold can gravitate toward the dark side of life. This would be unfortunate, for gold's function is to radiate love, compassion, and understanding to all who come into contact with its radiant light.

Through the characteristic expressions of the seven colors of Newton's spectrum and the higher octaves of the colors red and orange, we can gain a greater understanding of the true significance of colors and their effects upon us psychologically. Let us recognize that everything in life progresses from the dense material toward the ethereal or spiritual. In evolution we talk of man's continual progression through the trials of experience to reach a level where the divine spark latent within is ignited and his heritage of being created in the image of God is realized. As our colors progress through the color spectrum, the same process occurs. From the color red with its energy focused solely on the physical aspects of life we move through the spectrum to the violet end where the focus is upon the spiritual aspects of life. To reiterate the steps on this color ladder, let us recall briefly the function of each of these colors.

In red we have pure physical energy, the spontaneous manifestation of life. After red we move to orange, where there is a blending of red and yellow. Orange has a joy of living, unrestricted by reason yet limited to boundaries enforced by the initial stirring of the intellect. Yellow is the intellect, providing man with the mental faculties to reason. From yellow we reach the mid-point of the color spectrum at green. Through green the balance in nature is indicated. Green seeks purpose in manifestation and creates forms and structures. Beyond green we head toward the more spiritually oriented side of the spectrum. Blue is the serenity and peace resulting from faith in something beyond the mere physical form. This initial understanding of the depths of life continues to unfold as we move to indigo. Indigo integrates this awareness of life into its being. No longer is faith solely relied upon, but intuition becomes the foundation stone for attaining balance and harmony in the life process. This balance is not the balance of physical forms, as in green, but the balance of the physical and spiritual harmoniously united. At violet there is a stripping away of the desires of physical life. Violet has absorbed its experiences and digested its knowledge to transcend the passions and frustrations of physical life. These are the seven colors of Newton's spectrum. Each has its positive manner of expression and each one its negative. Toward the red end of the spectrum the energies are more materially oriented. Toward the violet end, more spiritually oriented. Either side can be lacking in the positive qualities of the other side. The red side can have no conception of the spiritual, while the violet side can separate itself from reality to live in its visions.

Progressing further, we dealt with the two colors we termed rose and gold. As mentioned previously, our use of these colors is based upon our intent to synthesize color and numbers which will offer us a technique for self-analysis and a possible means to improve conditions in our lives. In the number seven we have the cycle of earthly conditions. In the number nine we have the cycle of the dynamics of process. When we move from our seven-tiered cycle of color to our nine-tiered cycle of number, we arrive initially at rose, a color similar to red but of a higher octave. Rose directs red's driving energy toward creating realities out of the visions of others. Rose merges the infinitude of the spiritual with the finite of the material. From rose we move to the higher octave of orange, gold. Gold represents the end to the cycle of the dynamics of process. The light of wisdom shines for all. Evident through example and through sharing, gold expresses the perfect beauty of life.

We have seen the colors as real life energies and perhaps each of us is now more aware of the significance of the colors. Although we may better understand the meanings of colors, we need to learn to use these colors consciously. Already we can do so by our increased comprehension of their individual functions. Yet as each color vibrates at a different frequency, as each color has a different purpose, so too do we as individual human beings each function differently. Each of us has a different meaning to our lives. However, because of the conformity imposed by our learned responses, by society's standards, we too often incorrectly assume that we are all the same. We believe our lives to be identical, our functions to be similar, our hopes and frustrations shared by all. And when something comes along to upset this conception of total identity, we wonder, "Well then, who am I?", "What is my purpose here?" Unless we can come up with a convincing answer for ourselves, we become perplexed and discouraged. Eventually, from this confusion and despair comes the prodding for us to discover who we are. Through becoming more aware of ourselves, we can become more confident of our abilities and a greater peace with life. Let us proceed then to see how colors and numbers can offer us meaningful insights into our own being. If we can discover parts of ourselves through this rainbow spectrum, who could possibly ask for a greater pot of gold?

Chapter 5

The Colors in Your Rainbow

In our discussion of color to date we have learned that all color is contained in white light. From the totality of light we divide and differentiate into the component rays of color. When passed through a prism, light is broken down or refracted into the seven colors of the spectrum. We can now recognize color to be the product of the difference in refraction, as differences in the wavelengths of the rays, as differences in vibration. With dissimilar wavelengths individual color rays have diverse functions and distinctive characteristics. Rays with longer wavelengths have been seen as more physical, more material. The faster the wavelength of the color ray, the closer it approaches pure energy. As pure energy is approached, the emphasis is placed more upon the spiritual or non-corporeal aspects and less upon the material or physical factors. Already we have discussed the reality of color to such an extent that each one of us should be able to begin to consciously use the ever-present tool of color to better our states of being.

As we have mentioned repeatedly, all life is vibratory. Within the form of any tangible, living object is the latency of force. We have seen this reality in our own bodies with the discussion of the electric body, emanating from our physical body. Others have called it the aura or the etheric double, but in order not to confuse ourselves with mystical jargon we have called it the electric body and defined it as the energy of the individual not totally contained within the body but rather "spilling over" or radiating out from the physical body. We have explained the vibrancy of numbers with the totality being divided into differentiation and eventually through the continuation of variety into multiplicity. In the third chapter we analyzed the specific numbers 2, 3, and 7, in order to stress the significance of vibration and function in numbers. As different colors are related to diverse wavelengths and varying functions, so too do numbers represent diverse frequencies and varying functions. Numbers present us with symbols by which we can express the relationship of structures. Life is not only vibratory but structured and ordered, as well. Through this ordering process all life can be seen as mathematical relationships.

This perception of the order to life was expressed by Pythagoras, the sixth century B.C. Greek philosopher. Through his studies Pythagoras learned of the relationship between musical notes and numerical ratios. The awareness of this correlation led Pythagoras to develop the theory that all life could be expressed in numerical relationships. In the third chapter we began to understand the universal and all-inclusive correlations between life facts and numbers. When we described the specific colors, we were working not only with the characteristics of color but also those of number. As everything in the universe is scalar, so too are its component parts. Given below are the parallels between the colors and the numbers. Although we will be dealing with this correspondence to a greater extent through our self-analysis technique, recognize the reciprocity existing between number and color.

COLOR	NUMBER
red	1
orange	2
yellow	3
green	4
blue	5
indigo	6
violet	7
rose	8
gold	9

The mathematical relationships in life have fascinated many people. Since the time of Pythagoras people have continued to explore the significance and use of number. As a result, the sciences of mathematics and physics have evolved a greater understanding of life phenomena, engineers and architects have depended upon mathematical ratios in their work, and businessmen and government officials have employed the mathematics of statistical probability for forecasting purposes. Throughout our daily life mathematical structures constantly remind us of the ratios to living. In what is termed numerology the mathematical relationships between letters and numbers are used as a tool to increase the individual's understanding of himself. Based upon the recognition of life being vibratory and ordered in related structures, numerology offers a means by which we can become more aware of ourselves.

Where numerology proves deficient is in its inability to synthesize correlated studies and structures to the information the numbers reveal. In numerology we learn the significance of our name and birthdate to indicate basic characteristics regarding our potentials, our weaknesses, our purposes—our selves. While we become aware of such features of our being through numerology, we are left in a form of stasis with an inability to work with the life energies that surround us. Through correlating number with color we have the means by which we can work with these pulsating energies on a daily basis and use these energies in a constructive manner. Numerology, taken by itself, cannot provide us this opportunity. No doubt, by becoming more aware of ourselves we can more consciously work with the energies affecting us from both within and without. Where the problem arises is in considering these energies as fixed entities. At birth our name and our birthdate are fixed, thereby concretizing the energies of vibration within us. But numerologists do afford the individual the right to change his vibration or frequency rapport by changing his name. Although we cannot change our birthdate, we can change our name. Such a change, however, should be considered somewhat radical. For even though numerologists insist a name change can help the individual focus on energies beneficial to a harmonious blending of the whole, realize that the name given at birth will always have some bearing upon the individual.

Why, you might ask. Possibly we can find the answer through the spiritual teachings. Although mankind is presently wandering helplessly in a quandry of self-doubt and meaninglessness, man has a function to perform while on this earth plane. The purpose is not to build empires of forms that eventually decay and crumble. Nor is it merely to get and hoard all that one can during a stipulated time period. Rather, the purpose of man's living seems to be to evolve in consciousness, to perfect the qualities of one's own individual being, to transmute the passions and desires formed through the unconscious belief in finalities. To evolve is not to follow the precepts or standards of others. Instead it is necessary for us to be true to our essential selves. Each of us has different functions in living. And each of us must try to perform, to the best of our abilities, these functions. In the teachings of the ancient wisdom it is recognized that each individual picks the space-time coordinates conducive to the development of the necessary lessons he or she intends to learn during this cycle of earthly existence. The spiritualists assert that we pick our parents, we select our earthly conditions, we choose the environment best suited to our growth in character. During the process of becoming-being each of us has our own individual lessons to learn. Through a greater self-awareness we no longer need to learn the lessons of others as imposed upon us by parents, school, friends, society. With such tools as astrology,, numerology, and palmistry we can better understand ourselves. However, if we are going to maintain a fatalistic outlook on life, self-awareness alone will not help us to grow. We all know people mired in fatalism. Rather than take responsibility for their actions, they bemoan the conditions in which they find themselves. Instead of performing the function of conscious evolution with their life conditions as a backdrop, they despair of life, prompting themselves to stagnate, decay, and eventually die. For the life within such people has not been nourished. Like the snuffing of a candle they neglect and lose sight of the divine spark, that light within each one of us which shines dimly at first and then brighter as one struggles through the tunnel of space-time. Before the individual can truly evolve, he must recognize his own responsibility to correct the flaws and develop the qualities of his character. Once man accepts this responsibility for his own growth, then the quest for increased self-awareness begins. Who am I? he asks. What am I doing here? How can I make optimum use of the opportunities and the challenges of my life situation?

Through this searching, man strives. No longer content to sit back and let others care for him, as if he were but a caged animal, he goes out to discover the true. With self-awareness he begins to understand himself.

Not the person others think he is, not the person others would mold him to be, but the person he is. Conscious of his potentials and characteristics, the man can grow. As he begins to grow, he recognizes that he is not alone. He is surrounded by people, by conditions, by lessons—by energy. In learning about the all-pervasiveness of energy in the myriad of forms, the man can start to handle these energies in contrast to his previous behavior of merely reacting to the dynamics of a situation. And again we return to our concept of the synthesis of color and number. For through the reciprocity between color and number we gain the ability to consciously focus upon and direct the energies necessary for our continual development. By studying our name and our birthdate through the color-number analysis, we have a means by which we can learn about the energies predominant in us, the energies lacking within us, and the conscious use of these energies in our daily functioning. From the number-colors of our own being we can discover our level of vibration.

Does this truly sound so esoteric? Do you really question the concept of words as having differentiated vibrations? Perhaps you do, for it is an understanding we lose sight of as we take our use of language for granted. But consider, if you will, the fact that our language, our phrases, our names, are but structured relationships of sounds. Remember your experience of learning words as a child. Or, if you are privileged to have young children of your own, see it in their own development of speech. To children there is an awe and wonder to all of life. Life is a continuously fresh experience. There is a newness to life that time and assumed repetition have yet to make boring. So recall the learning of language in school. The sounds of words are focused upon. Language is exaggerated. The syllable sounds are stressed. Take the time now to focus your awareness on the sounds of the following words. Don't even consider the meanings of the words. But concentrate upon the sounds. Exaggerate them, stress them, elongate the tonal qualities of these words.

RAGE

CHEERY

SAD

These words sound different, don't they? Rage doesn't sound like cheery. Nor does sad sound like rage. Each of these words has different tonal qualities, based upon the structured relationship of the letters and consequently the sounds or vibrations. The frequencies of these words are different, similar to the difference of our color rays or our numbers. The same is true of our names. Someone with the name Bernard Baruch sounds different from someone with the name Jorge Luis Borges. And the same is true of our own individual names. Each name has a different vibration or frequency to it. Through our names we have a means to differentiate one another. If I were to go to an airport and page on the public address system for "John David Stevenson," would many people respond? While some might listen to hear what the message said, only John David Stevenson is likely to take the time to check on the page. Our name is one of our marks of individuality, and according to the numerologists our name and our birthdate are among the conditions we select in order to learn our lessons in life. Through the vibration of our name and birthdate we incorporate and surround ourselves with certain energies for our character development. Let us then consider the different aspects to our name and see how through a synthesis of number and color we can find a means not only to increase our self-awareness but to improve our states of being.

To begin with, we need to construct the table of letters and their correspondence to the nine numbers and colors we will be using.

101

COLOR	NUMBER	LETTERS		
RED	1	A	J	S
ORANGE	2	B	K	T
YELLOW	3	C	L	U
GREEN	4	D	M	V
BLUE	5	E	N	W
INDIGO	6	F	O	X
VIOLET	7	G	P	Y
ROSE	8	H	Q	Z
GOLD	9	I	R	

In our work with color-number analysis in this book we will concentrate upon several major aspects revealed in the name. And in our study let us remember the possibility, according to the spiritualists the reality of conscious deliberation, that each of us picks our own name. If we can understand ourselves to be living forms containing vibrant forces alternating at various frequencies, then is it truly so far off to imagine ourselves vibrating to a verbal sound which is linked to our living frequency vibration? After all, in many techniques of meditation a sound is used as the vibratory tool to attune oneself to the vibration of meditation. The mantra or chanting of sounds has long been used as a means of alignment to cosmic forces.

In the total name of the individual, as given at birth, we have an indication of the basic qualities of character in that person. Let us assume we have a fictional guest with us by the name of John Smith Doe. Interested in the color-number technique, Mr. Doe asks us to correlate the letters in his name to the numbers and colors. Mr. Doe gives us his full name at birth as John Smith Doe. To find the *expression* of the individual we numerate *all* the letters in his name and then add them together until we get a single digit number.

If we have a two-digit number, e.g., 59, we reduce this number by adding 5 + 9, and get 14. As we still have a two-digit number, we reduce this number by adding 1 + 4, to eventually arrive at 5. We now have one single-digit number.

```
J O H N   S M I T H   D O E
1 6 8 5   1 4 9 2 8   4 6 5
```

$$20 \ + \ 24 \ + \ 15 \ = 59$$
$$5+9 = 14$$
$$1+4 = 5, \text{blue}$$

This gives us the expression of John Smith Doe to be a number 5, the color blue. The full name represents the contact point of the individual with the world. The color of the full name indicates the way the person relates to other people. It is the person's calling card, what he appears to be. It can also denote the functions and tasks the person may be called upon to perform in the outside world. Through the full name we learn the potentials and possibilities that await the person who is willing to develop his talents and correct his frailties, both of which will be designated by the color. For while energy is pure in the sense of being totally objective, energies can be handled in either positive or negative ways in accord with the energy level of the individual working with these energies.

In the full name of our guest, John Smith Doe, we have the potential for the expression of blue in both constructive and destructive manners. Look back to the last chapter and recall the description of the characteristics of blue. There will be times when Mr. Doe, who places great faith in the security of his inner peace, will be jolly and fazed by nothing. Other times, Mr. Doe will vacillate, unable to decide what to do with his energies and thereby flitting from one thing to another, never seeing anything through to completion. Now aware of the characteristics of his manner of expression to the world, Mr. Doe may be better able to concentrate on the positive qualities of blue and to defuse the negative before they grab control of his behavior.

As we continue through life, we use other names to express ourselves to the world. Although the full name given at birth represents the basic, underlying mode of expression for Mr. Doe, any change to the full name reveals the function or purpose he may be expressing at that period in his life. For instance, our fictional guest has told me of the different full names he has used and been known by. As he grew up, he was known as Johnny Doe. Later he used John S. Doe, then J.S. Doe and is presently calling himself John Doe. At different periods in time Mr. Doe has vibrated to energies of different character and function. As he presently uses the name John Doe, let us find his most recent mode of expression. To do so, we numerate the letters of John Doe and find the sum.

$$J O H N \quad D O E$$
$$1 6 8 5 \quad 4 6 5$$

$$20 \; + \; 15 \; = 35$$
$$3+5=8, \text{ rose}$$

John Doe is now vibrating to a number 8, the rose color, in his expression. The faith and devotion, inherently a part of his blue, may be presently seeking expression through John Doe's encounters with large-scale enterprises. The freedom needed by blue may have an outlet through rose's ability to organize, administer and direct the ideas of others into concrete results. We should also be aware of the negative aspects of the rose expression. Mr. Doe could be overbearing in his approach, trying to have everyone submit to his authority. Through knowing the characteristics of blue and rose, Mr. Doe has the capability to control patterns of behavior instigated by the frequency of his living vibration. While his own name changes may be transitory, his full name at birth will always color the full names he uses as he grows through life. For John Smith Doe the two colors predominant in his present expression are blue and rose. By focusing on these colors or by using them in coloring the externals of his life, John Doe can more accurately line up his energies to operate in constructive ways.

However, we should also see where our guest is lacking energy. Again we look to the full name. Having seen the gestalt of expression in John Smith Doe, we are now interested in the microcosm of the name, or the component parts that go into creating the name. Therefore, we will dissect the full name and look at the individual colors contained in the name. In this analysis we will be looking for a balance. Where there are certain energies lacking within us, we should be aware of these energies. By an increased recognition of our lacks and areas of overemphasis, we can consciously balance off the energies by our working with them. Let us then examine the question of balance in John Smith Doe.

			colors in the full name	
J	1	red		
O	6	indigo		
H	8	rose		
N	5	blue	red	2
			orange	1
S	1	red	yellow	0
M	4	green	green	2
I	9	gold	blue	2
T	2	orange	indigo	2
H	8	rose	violet	0
			rose	2
D	4	green	gold	1
O	6	indigo		
E	5	blue		

In John Smith Doe we find a fairly equitable balance between the nine colors of our scale. The colors totally lacking in John Smith Doe indicate the deficient energies. Look back to chapter three and see how the lack of yellow and violet might affect John Smith Doe. The intellect and reasoning faculties might seem less attuned, and there would seem to be a need to sharpen the curiosity and delve below surface appearances. Reason could be lacking in some of John Smith Doe's actions. By returning to Newton's seven-tiered color spectrum, we would see the emphasis placed upon the red and the rose, the higher octave of red. Red and rose make up four of the twelve letters in the name, or one third of the total. The physical energy of red and the organizational abilities of rose seem strengthened. Isn't it interesting that our guest presently calls himself John Doe, thereby stressing the rose energy in his expression? Within the full name as given at birth the rose is well accounted for and accentuated in strength by the red. It seems John Doe has unconsciously decided to emphasize in his expression an energy that is a large part of his inherent makeup. But let us continue with our exploration of balance and see how it manifests in the presently used name of John Doe.

			colors in the name	
J	1	red	red	1
O	6	indigo	orange	0
H	8	rose	yellow	0
N	5	blue	green	1
			blue	2
D	4	green	indigo	2
O	6	indigo	violet	0
E	5	blue	rose	1
			gold	0

In John Doe blue and indigo are the dominant individual rays. Remember the expression of John Smith Doe, his name as given at birth, was blue. Even though his present expression of rose has a different function than blue, the blue is still strong within the name. This emphasis both upon blue and indigo would modify the rose expression. Dependent upon his functioning level of consciousness, John Doe's approach to dealing with the world would seem to be one of great confidence whether in himself, in a force he might call God, or in the supposed blind hands of fate. The red-rose combination also has two of the seven colors in the present expression. Joined to blue's depth of faith and devotion and indigo's desire to serve others through adjusting problems, red-rose would add the motivation and ability to administer and concentrate on the practical realities of life. Therefore, John Doe may present himself to the world as capable and compassionate, as an individual worthy of the trust of friends and the responsibility of authority, as a man with a determination to achieve. Where the balance is lacking is in the orange, yellow, violet, and gold. Our guest should be aware that because of the absence of the joyous colors of orange, yellow, and gold, he may also display a rather serious, reserved nature. At times John Doe may feel as if the responsibility he wants and works for is in actual fact too much for him to cope with. From the lack of yellow and violet he will still tend to jump into things without considering the possible consequences of his actions. As he may rely too heavily on his driving will and his faith in intuitive hunches, he should consciously focus upon his mental faculties and upon reasoning out his course of action. These would be several of the probable ways for John Doe to express himself.

Let us look further into the character of John Smith Doe. We have seen the mode of expression, his contact with the world, to be inherently blue (5) with his present expression rose (8). Now we shall explore the *inner urge* of John Smith Doe—that motivating factor for him to perform certain tasks, to live in a definite manner, to be the kind of person he is. This inner urge shows what the individual wants to be or wants to do. Found through the vowels (A—E—I—O—U) contained in the name, we find the motivating factor in the case of our guest to be rose, the number 8.

```
J
O     6    indigo
H
N

S
M                    6+9+6+5=26
I     9    gold                2+6=8, rose
T
H

D
O     6    indigo
E     5    blue
```

Consider the characteristics of the color rose. We would learn that John Smith Doe's primary inner urge is to construct dreams into realities, the need to control, to guide, to direct. It is interesting to note John Smith Doe's inner urge has the same function as his present form of expression. The motivating factor within has become the expression without. Often when one changes name, not only does the mode of expression change but so too·does the inner urge. Although the inner urge of the name given at birth will always have an underlying influence, the motivating force behind a person's actions can change in life. In John Doe we see his present inner urge has not changed but is still rose, the number 8.

```
J
O     6    indigo
H
N                        6+6+5=17
                             1+7=8, rose
D
O     6    indigo
E     5    blue
```

John Doe's primary focus would likely be on some form of management and organization. Not only is the underlying inner urge consistent with the present motivational factor, but both are congruent with the present expression. In passing, we should also check the contents of the inner urge and see if one color is dominant. As we find indigo, the number 6, to be the strongest individual color in the inner urges of both John Smith Doe and John Doe, we should recognize that part of his motivational factor will be influenced by the color indigo. He may have a deep urge to create a balanced and secure environment around himself. His home is likely to be open to all, but with rose as the inner urge totality he is likely to expect others who enter into his world to recognize his authority. Besides the desire to direct his energies toward specific goals, John Doe needs to establish a secure base of operations conducive to harmony. Through our colors we have briefly described the inner urges behind John Smith Doe's and John Doe's actions.

Apart from the expression and the inner urge of the individual, we are also interested in analyzing the individual when he is alone without the need to excel, to compete, to present himself to others. Termed the *latent self*, this characteristic shows the person at rest, the daydreaming qualities of the person. Ascertained through the summing up of the consonants in the name, the latent self in our guest, John Smith Doe, is indigo, the number 6.

J	1	red
O		
H	8	rose
N	5	blue
S	1	red
M	4	green
I		
T	2	orange
H	8	rose
D	4	green
O		
E		

$$1+8+5+1+4+2$$
$$+8+4=33$$
$$3+3=6, \text{indigo}$$

When John Smith Doe is alone by himself without the need to strive, his attitude toward life is one of an indigo function. Recall that contained within the rose color of the inner urges of John Smith Doe and John Doe there is a strong emphasis of indigo. Now we see indigo as the expression of John Smith Doe when he is at rest. It is, therefore, likely that John Smith Doe tries to maintain a degree of harmony in his life, seeks to balance the dual aspects of life, and enjoys the comfort of his home. When considering the individual components in the latent self, we find the colors red and green accentuated. The red here underlines much of the red-rose involved in his daily expression and inner urges. The green offers a balancing between the causative forces and resultant material forms in life. In John Smith Doe's situation the green and red within the latent self would probably combine to direct the energy and drive into the construction of forms and systems. Green is likely to channel red towards a constructive outlet of energy, perhaps toward a functioning similar to rose, where energy is used to build concrete forms from visions. As John Smith Doe strives to obtain executive roles in his life incidents, recognize the latent self and the dominant components of both the natal and present inner urges to be related to the indigo function of adjusting situations to attain balance and harmony. Similar to our process of study with the other divisions of analysis, we also look at the latent self as presently expressed in John Doe.

J	1	red
O		
H	8	rose
N	5	blue
D	4	green
O		
E		

$1+8+5+4=18$

$1+8=9$, gold

At present, John Doe's latent self vibrates to the gold frequency. Remember the characteristics of the gold function. A degree of perfection is sought, where the balance of harmony has been realized. Although there are times in his contact with the world when John Doe's expression may be reserved, shy, and rather austere, it is likely that in the security of his home he is warm and affectionate with friends and acquaintances alike. What John Doe has earned through the labors of the rose function is being harvested. A radiance shines forth. Wanting to share with others, John Doe sows through example the joy of living in the hearts of others. In the individual components of John Doe's latent self we see colors that appear prominently in various categories of analysis of John Smith Doe's character.

Another factor considered in the color self-analysis technique is the birthdate. Similar to the science of astrology, where configurations of planetary energies at birth produce the psychological patterns necessary for the entering individual to learn various lessons, develop their potentials, and correct their frailties, so too does numerology understand the birthdate to be a vibratory frequency of function. In numerology the birthdate represents the life path or destiny of the person. The areas needing attention during this lifetime are indicated by the birthdate. The birthdate tells of the individual's environment, the external surroundings in which the individual will use his expression, inner urges, and latent self to grow in character. It provides information regarding the vocational aptitudes and those realms where the individual may have the opportunity to express himself. When considering the birthdate, we numerate the months in the following manner:

January	1
February	2
March	3
April	4
May	5
June	6
July	7
August	8
September	9
October	10 = 1
November	11 = 2
December	12 = 3

In the case of our fictional guest, John Smith Doe, we have a birthdate of September 9, 1934, which gives us a life path of rose, the number 8.

September 9, 1934

$$9 \qquad 9 \quad 1934 = 9+9+1+9+3+4 = 35$$
$$3+5 = 8, \text{rose}$$

The environment, the tasks to be performed during this life period, relate to the rose function. Already we have seen the pervasiveness of the rose function in John Smith Doe. It has been indicated in the present expression of John Doe, in the components of the natal expression, in the inner urges, in the components of the latent self, and now in the vibration of his surroundings. There can be little doubt that John Smith Doe's efforts will have a conducive environment for successful results. After all, John Smith Doe is living within a realm of large-scale enterprises, of organization and management. His own urges and expressions are strongly related to this environment, and, therefore, he is likely to encounter little resistance to effective functioning in his endeavors.

Through the correspondence of number and color, we have devised a quick character analysis of John Smith Doe. We have seen him as an energetic individual, desirous of achieving results. His inclination toward peace and harmony necessitates the comforts of home, family, and security. His inexhaustible drive serves as the motivation to do things in a big way, to create structures from ideas, to organize and administer. Through the lack of yellow and violet we know the missing energies in John Doe and would caution our guest to take more time to reason things out, to look into the details of situations, to further his objectives through considered judgment rather than hunches and physical drive. Although we are now aware of many aspects of John Smith Doe's character, the question might arise as to what he can do with this knowledge. As we have synthesized the function of number and color, we have constructed a tool to use these energies in everyday living. Conscious of the functions of each color, and now aware of his own life patterns, John Smith Doe can color his world in such a way as to accentuate his strengths of character and to control or correct his weaknesses. In the next section we will deal extensively with the practical use of color in our daily lives. But for now, each of us is ready to devise our own color rainbow. To reiterate the procedure of analysis let us take another example and briefly run through the process. In this case, we will deal with a fictional woman by the name of Constance Everly Browne, born on January 3, 1943.

To begin our color analysis of Constance Everly Browne we look to her *expression*, which we find by

113

numerating all the letters in the full name given at birth
and reducing the value to a single digit.

```
C O N S T A N C E   E V E R L Y   B R O W N E
3 6 5 1 2 1 5 3 5   5 4 5 9 3 7   2 9 6 5 5 5
```

$$31 \quad + \quad 33 \quad + \quad 32 \quad = 96$$
$$9+6=15$$
$$1+5=6,$$
indigo

The expression of Constance Everly Browne is that
of indigo, the number 6. In considering how she might
present herself to the outside world, we would recall
the characteristics of indigo. When we reflect on indigo,
let us remember that while energy is pure it can be used
in either constructive or destructive ways. As both the
positive and the negative aspects of indigo are within
her expression, it is Ms. Browne's responsibility to focus
upon the positive and control the negative.

After we study the expression, we note the balancing
of the energies that comprise the expression. We dissect
the full name into its component colors and in our
example find the following representation:

red	orange	yellow	green	blue	indigo	violet	rose	gold
2	2	3	1	8	2	1	0	2

Accentuated within the expression of Constance
Everly Browne is the blue function, whose strength
could lead to an overemphasis. Knowledgeable of the
characteristics of blue, Ms. Browne should be wary of
times when the blue function may dominate her indigo
expression. Where she is lacking energy is in the colors
of rose, violet, and green. Through conscious focusing
on these three colors she can balance off the missing
energies within her expression.

As we progress through life, we sometimes change

the names we are known by. At such times we vibrate to different frequencies and different functions. Let us see this effect in Constance Everly Browne's name changes. When she was growing up, she was known as Connie Browne. At that period in time her mode of expression was vibrating to the orange function, the number 2.

$$\begin{array}{c} \text{C O N N I E} \quad \text{B R O W N E} \\ \text{3 6 5 5 9 5} \quad \text{2 9 6 5 5 5} \end{array}$$

$$33 \quad + \quad 32 \quad = 65$$
$$6+5=11$$
$$1+1=2, \text{ orange}$$

If we were specifically interested in dealing with that time in her life, we would dissect the orange expression into its integral parts to witness the balancing of energies. However, our primary interest is to deal with her inherent mode of expression, as given by her birth name, and her recent expression, as denoted by the name she uses presently. Therefore, let us continue. After college Connie Browne married George Lester and became known as Constance Browne Lester, her maiden name supplanting her given middle name of Everly. By marriage she changed her daily expression from the orange-indigo combination to the violet-indigo combination. (Recognize the indigo function to be her inherent mode of expression, which will always influence any periodic manner of expression.)

```
C O N S T A N C E   B R O W N E   L E S T E R
3 6 5 1 2 1 5 3 5   2 9 6 5 5 5   3 5 1 2 5 9
```

31   +   32   +   25   =88
$$8+8=16$$
$$1+6=7,$$
violet

In passing, let us observe that in marrying George Lester, her expression became that of the violet function, an energy lacking in her natal expression. Yet Constance Browne Lester is known today as Connie Lester and as a result her expression is green, another energy lacking in her natal expression.

```
C O N N I E   L E S T E R
3 6 5 5 9 5   3 5 1 2 5 9
```

33   +   25   =58
$$5+8=13$$
$$1+3=4, \text{ green}$$

Concerned with her present manner of expression, we consider the balance within the green expression.

red	orange	yellow	green	blue	indigo	violet	rose	gold
1	1	2	0	5	1	0	0	2

The balancing of energies within her present expression is quite similar to the components in her natal expression: a strong blue function and deficient energies in the green, violet, and rose functions. After we explain to Ms. Lester the areas of strength and weakness in her expression, as shown by the color analysis, we move on to her inner urges.

The *inner urge* is found by numerating the vowels and reducing their sum to a single digit. From her name given at birth we discover her motivation to be of the indigo function, the number 6.

```
CONSTANCE  EVERLY  BROWNE
6    1   5 5 5        6    5
```

$$12 \quad + \quad 10 \quad + \quad 11 \quad = 33$$
$$3+3=6,$$
indigo

After considering the effects of the indigo function on her inner urge, we regard the similarity in function between her natal expression and her natal inner urge. Next we move to her present inner urge, as revealed by the vowels in Connie Lester. We find her inner urge at present relates to the yellow function, the number 3.

```
CONNIE  LESTER
6     9 5   5    5
```

$$20 \quad + \quad 10 \quad = 30$$
$$3+0=3, \text{ yellow}$$

Having found, studied and compared her inner urges and her expressions, we look to the *latent self* of Constance Everly Browne. Indicating the person alone and at rest, the latent self is found by numerating the consonants and reducing the value to a single digit. In Constance Everly Browne the latent self is gold, the number 9.

```
CONSTANCE  EVERLY  BROWNE
3 512 53    4 937 29  55
```

$$19 \quad + \quad 23 \quad + \quad 21 \quad = 63$$
$$6+3=9,$$
gold

Then we look to her present latent self and find Connie Lester to be vibrating to the red function, the number 1.

CONNIE LESTER
3 55   3 12 9

$$13 \quad + \quad 15 \quad = 28$$
$$2+8 = 10$$
$$1+0 = 1, \text{red}$$

Once we have examined the latent self in both Constance Everly Browne and Connie Lester, related the latent self to her expressions and inner urges, and considered the totality and the components of all aspects of the names, we proceed to learn of Constance Everly Browne's *destiny*, as shown by her birthdate. Born January 3, 1943, we find Constance Everly Browne's environment to be one of the yellow function, the number 3.

January 3, 1943
1   3 1943 $= 1+3+1+9+4+3 = 21$
$$2+1 = 3, \text{yellow}$$

Through the synthesis of color and number, we have possibly composed a quite accurate analysis of Connie Lester, born Constance Everly Browne. Through knowledge of the functions of color, we can offer Connie Lester a greater awareness of her character: not only her strengths and potentials but her weaknesses and possible areas of difficulty. By imparting to her an understanding of the colors necessary to both balance off her own energies and emphasize qualities that are seeking fuller expression, we can direct her toward a more conscious use of energy.

Now that we have made Connie Lester more aware of herself, how about you? Through two examples we have explained the method of investigation for our color self-analysis technique. Therefore, you should have little trouble in analyzing yourself. After you have completed the mechanics of analysis, re-read chapter four to familiarize yourself with the characteristics and functions of the nine colors. In the following chapter we will deal more extensively with the interpretation of our analysis. In order for all of us to understand the process of interpretation, the next chapter is devoted to the study of four well-known personalities.

Chapter 6

The Rainbows of the Stars

In the last chapter we explained the mechanics to the process of analysis through our color-number technique. Using the examples of John Smith Doe and Constance Everly Browne, we learned the method to find the expression, the inner urge, the latent self, the balancing of energies, and the destiny of any individual. By a change in their name we saw how people can alter certain aspects of their character, placing emphasis upon functions other than those they were born with. Although name changes affect the expression, the inner urge and latent self of the individual, we discovered the destiny, based upon the birthdate, to be the one aspect of character that could never change. We delineated the meanings of the various characteristics in the individual. For John Doe we discussed the different color functions of his character. With the mechanics completed and with insights into the interpretation of the analysis given, the reader was urged to compose his own color rainbow.

But did you? Or did you shrug off the color-number analysis technique with the impatience of skepticism, justifying your attitude with the belief that because you had never met John Doe or Connie Lester, you were unable to appreciate any potential benefit in the technique? While the color-number technique might prove helpful in increasing your awareness of your self, it can only do so if you are willing to give it a fair trial by actually working the technique and judging the validity of the rainbow it devises for you.

In order to demonstrate the application of the color-number technique to real life, this chapter is devoted to a brief, concise interpretation of the color rainbows of four well-known personalities. The reader can then decide about the relevancy of our technique, and with greater faith in its potential you can construct your own color rainbow.

The first celebrity to be analyzed through our color-number technique is a woman who has shown an incomparable degree of strength and elegance during the times of triumph and tragedy which have been so much a part of her life. Since Eleanor Roosevelt, no American woman has had such an impact upon the world as our subject of study, Jacqueline Lee Bouvier. Born July 28, 1929, Ms. Bouvier has been the wife of the American President John F. Kennedy and the wife of the Greek entrepreneur Aristotle Onassis. In our study we will look at three periods in her life: as a young girl prior to her marriage to John Kennedy, as Mrs. John Kennedy, and as Mrs. Aristotle Onassis. To begin with, let us find the colors which will always be a part of her expression, as found through the colors in her name given at birth.

```
J A C Q U E L I N E   L E E   B O U V I E R
1 1 3 8 3 5 3 9 5 5   3 5 5   2 6 3 4 9 5 9 = 94 = 13 = 4,
                                               green
```

Ms. Bouvier's expression is green, the number 4. Remember the expression of the individual reflects the way people present themselves to the world. With green as her expression we would expect Ms. Bouvier to appear to the world as a young woman involved with the material aspects of life. Born of a wealthy family, Ms. Bouvier was virtually the prototype of a socially prominent young lady. Her family lived in New York and summered in the Hamptons on Long Island. Like many young ladies of her social breeding, she was fond of horseback riding, educated at private schools, and presented to society as a debutante. Who could argue that Ms. Bouvier's upbringing seems to have been the traditional pattern of a young woman of her background?

But recall that green seeks a purpose for its life. Being immersed in the growth and continual renewal of nature, green seeks the means to effect ideas into form. True to the function of her green expression, Ms. Bouvier was not content merely to be a social matron but sought outlets by which she could grow and develop her character. Before we concern ourselves with the forms her creativity took, we will look at the components of her expression to discover the dominant colors and colors lacking. The components will give us an idea as to how her expression was modified and the possible channels for her expression.

COLORS IN JACQUELINE LEE BOUVIER

red	orange	yellow	green	blue	indigo	violet	rose	gold
2	1	5	1	6	1	0	1	3

Within her expression of green we find the dominant colors to be blue and yellow with violet altogether absent. With yellow accented we would expect the intellect to be developed. Radiating the cheer of yellow, Ms. Bouvier would seem to enjoy working with her mind. In actual fact, Ms. Bouvier expressed her creative instincts in writing, both for her school paper and later for the *Washington Times-Herald*. Although she started her college career at Vassar, it seems the combination of an emphatic blue and an absent violet contributed to her decision to interrupt her studies at Vassar. As violet gives the impetus to delve into the substance of a subject, violet's absence would tend to limit concentrated study and allow for greater diversity. With blue there is always the possibility of having many irons in the fire and of roaming the four corners of the world in exploration. During her junior year of college Ms. Bouvier studied at the Sorbonne in Paris and upon return from her year abroad continued her studies at George Washington University.

When we consider the inner urge of Ms. Bouvier, we find her motivating factor to be orange, the number 2, which is the same characteristic as her latent self.

INNER URGE

```
  1    3 5  9  5    5 5   6 3  9 5  = 56 = 11 = 2,
J A C Q U E L I N E  L E E  B O U V I E R   orange
  1  3 8    3  5    3     2    4    9 = 38 = 11 = 2,
LATENT SELF                              orange
```

With orange as the function of both her inner urge and her latent self, there would seem in Ms. Bouvier the desire and need to go beyond the social necessities of her background and assert her individuality in a forceful yet reasoned manner. As orange balances the raw vitality of red and the mental intellect of yellow, so too does it emphasize the balance in life, an appreciation of form and of the esthetic. The orange function seems indicated in Ms. Bouvier's involvement in dance, participation in dramatics at school, and her interest in the cultural aspects of society. Orange also deals with relatedness with others, and in Ms. Bouvier we could expect charm and grace in her associations with others.

July 28, 1929, her birthdate, indicates her environment to be orange.

JULY 28, 1929
7+2+8+1+9+2+9=38=11=2, orange

Throughout her life, Ms. Bouvier, Mrs. Kennedy, Mrs. Onassis will have in her destiny the opportunity to cultivate her appreciation of the arts, to develop her individuality through associations with others, and to surround herself with the vibrant world of ideas and thought.

By becoming Jackie Kennedy, Ms. Bouvier changed the vibration of her expression and inner urge but not her latent self.

JACKIE KENNEDY
113295 2555547=54=9, gold

As Jackie Kennedy, her expression became that of gold, the number 9. In gold there is the radiance of a level of perfection attained, a shining forth of the spark within that comforts all who bask in its light. And who can deny the light Jackie Kennedy provided in her expression? Was she not aware of the beauty in life? Did she not translate this beauty to others through her interest in the arts, through her elegant manners in diplomatic circles, through her joy of living? Largely as a result of Jackie Kennedy, the Kennedy years in the White House have been called the Camelot years.

Camelot refers to the seat of power of King Arthur in the Arthurian legends. To the British Isles Arthur epitomized a level of consciousness analogous to that of the Christ. Britons for centuries spoke in eager anticipation of the second coming of Arthur. As the Christ had twelve disciples, Arthur's Round Table was composed of twelve knights, each of whom, according to occult lore, had a function to perform in perfecting individual qualities, in attaining the level of an Arthur, in realizing the divinity within.

During the short-lived period of the Kennedy years

in the United States mankind was offered a sparkle of hope, an emphasis upon what man could attain, an appreciation of what man had achieved through the endeavors of creative geniuses in the arts and sciences. During those thousand days, many Americans, in fact many world citizens, felt the new day dawning, a day to signal the heights man could scale, of the society that could be. Much of this sense of perfection emanated from Jackie Kennedy, as if she were cloaked in an aura of gold.

In her expression as Jackie Kennedy, blue, a strong factor in her expression as Jacqueline Lee Bouvier, again dominated the component colors.

COLORS IN JACKIE KENNEDY

red	orange	yellow	green	blue	indigo	violet	rose	gold
2	2	1	1	5	0	1	0	1

Perhaps in consequence of the indigo and rose energies missing in her expression as Jackie Kennedy, some people complained of her aloofness, of her being too detached, of not translating her feelings into practical realities. Yet we know gold's function is to serve through being, to share with others through example, and not the missionary function we might expect of the indigo color. Without the rose color in her expression there would not be the energy to construct, direct, and administer the dreams into realities for the benefit of all. Therefore, such criticism of Jackie Kennedy was totally unwarranted, for it demanded of her something she was not. As Jackie Kennedy her expression was one of involvement in life and through example to allow others to share the brilliancy of her being.

Her inner urge as Jackie Kennedy became the violet color, an energy totally lacking in her natal expression.

126

JACKIE KENNEDY
1   9 5   5   5   = 25 = 7, violet

With a violet inner urge we can more fully understand the motivation to create a "Camelot atmosphere"
in the White House. We know violet to be a light-
bringer. With violet, however, light is brought through
the striving to attain an ideal, as opposed to gold's
radiance through example. An inspired function, violet
gives man the masterworks in art, philosophy, and
science. Within Mrs. Kennedy it seems there was an
urge to bring to the awareness of the general public
the works of master creators. Through her cultivation
the arts were nurtured and given a platform in the
White House from which to enlighten the public. The
poise and refinement of violet can be seen in Mrs.
Kennedy, who served as the epitome of elegance and
intelligence in womanhood and, thus, gave faith to the
initial stirrings of the women's liberation movement. In
the violet inner urge one can perhaps understand the
basis for some of the criticism of her aloofness and her
detachment from mundane reality. For violet does have
a tendency to lose itself from reality in visions of perfection. Again we see this aura of Camelot around the
Kennedy White House years. Some could charge that
these so-called Camelot years were not so perfect but
were a mere escape from reality's problems. But
shouldn't we, at least, be thankful for the glimmer of
what could be? After all, from visions realities can be
made. And there can be no doubt that these years of
American history influenced a great number of people
with hope, joy, and the motivation to better our world.

As we mentioned previously, Jackie Kennedy re-
tained the orange function of her latent self, similar to
her latent self as Jacqueline Lee Bouvier.

```
J A C K I E   K E N N E D Y
1   3 2       2   5 5   4 7 = 29 = 11 = 2, orange
```

Her days as Jackie Kennedy, the wife of an American president, ended when her husband was shot down in Dallas. The world grieved, as the Camelot days ended. A new President took to the White House, and the mood of America changed.

The widowed Mrs. Kennedy eventually became Mrs. Aristotle Onassis. As Jackie Onassis her inner urge and latent self changed, while her expression of gold remained the same.

```
J A C K I E   O N A S S I S
1 1 3 2 9 5   6 5 1 1 1 9 1 = 45 = 9, gold
```

Although Jackie Onassis tried to escape the role of celebrity in order to lead a more private life, others refused her the right. She continued to express the gold function, and some demanded that she share this radiance with all. What is especially interesting in her expression as Jackie Onassis is the change in the color components of the expression.

COLORS IN JACKIE ONASSIS

red	orange	yellow	green	blue	indigo	violet	rose	gold
6	1	1	0	2	1	0	0	2

Red now became heavily accented. She became more individualistic, more self-oriented. Her life was to be her own. Yet others tried to deny her the privilege. Some probably acted out of the need to cling to the glimpse of Camelot that had been seen. But the magical kingdom had been overrun, and this fact was understood by Jackie Onassis, who reflected this attitude by the total absence of the violet energy in her expression. The changes to come in America were similar to the account given by Alfred, Lord Tennyson in his "Morte

D'Arthur." As Sir Bedivere places Arthur, seriously wounded at the Battle of Camlon, in a barge to be taken to the island of Avalon, Bedivere bids farewell to his lord:

"But now the whole Round Table is dissolved
Which was an image of the mighty world."

Not only is the violet energy missing in her expression as Jackie Onassis, but rose remains absent, suggesting once again that hers is not the function of guiding and directing others in large-scale endeavors. Although green is also lacking, we will find it to be her inner urge. By marrying Aristotle Onassis she gained the indigo energy with one of its characteristics being the importance placed upon the family.

Jackie Onassis's inner urge revolved around the green function, her expression as Jacqueline Lee Bouvier.

$$\begin{array}{cccccc}
\text{J A C K I E} & & \text{O N A S S I S} \\
1 & 9\,5 & 6 & 1 & 9 & =31=4, \text{green}
\end{array}$$

Her inner urge became more concerned with the security in mundane realities. As her own childhood expression was reinforced by her green inner urge, the growth and nourishment of her own children would seem a dominant motivation in her. It is also possible that some of her love nature had been crushed by tragedy, thereby leading her to seek a greater balance between the spiritual and physical aspects of life as opposed to her previous tendency to be influenced by the visions of possibilities. The peace and serenity of green might be sought. But life still needed a purpose. Perhaps initially she found that purpose in caring for her young children. Later, as her children approached adulthood, her purpose was reawakened to the interests of her childhood expression by her participation in the world of literature as a publishing house editor.

As Jackie Onassis her latent self vibrated to blue, a

function strong within her expression as both Jacqueline Lee Bouvier and Jackie Kennedy.

J A C K I E   O N A S S I S
1   3 2   5   1 1   1 = 14 = 5, blue

When alone by herself without the need to push forward, Jackie Onassis may have felt a strong desire to travel widely, to involve herself in many interests, to search for experiences by which she could understand more fully the depths of the life process. And always in her latent self there was the faith and devotion that had stood by her in times of trial and sorrow.

Such has been the life of Jacqueline Lee Bouvier, as seen through our color-number analysis. What the future holds for her is dependent upon her use of the energies. One might hope that she could get over some of the hurt, indicated by the withdrawal of the violet energy from her life expression. But it is her life, and she should be allowed, as should we all, to live it in accord with the manner in which she feels she can gain the greatest benefit. We can only thank her for what she has given us and wish her well as she continues to grow through life.

Few musicians can claim to have had such an impact upon music in the 1970s as has the subject of our second study, Reginald Kenneth Dwight. Born March 25, 1947, Dwight has become a superstar under the name of Elton John. In our brief color-number analysis of Elton John we will consider both his name given at birth and his stage name. At birth Reginald Kenneth Dwight vibrated to an expression of the orange function.

R E G I N A L D   K E N N E T H   D W I G H T
9 5 7 9 5 1 3 4   2 5 5 5 5 2 8   4 5 9 7 8 2 = 110 = 2,
                                                    orange

With orange as his expression we might expect Reginald Kenneth Dwight to present himself as a young man full of energy, determination, and mental curiosity. As orange is able to dissect situations into its component parts and blend the parts back into a balanced whole, music would seem to be a natural for him. The innate rhythm and timing of orange would give him both an appreciation of and ability in musical composition. Where he may have had a problem in growing up would be in orange's tendency to be too responsive to the opinions of others. Interested in relationships, orange can become overly concerned with the way others react to it. Fostered by this importance of other people's reactions, orange tends to be overly exacting in its demands upon itself, which can lead to a hypercritical attitude, a fear of failure, and consequent feelings of inferiority. An emotionally charged color, orange needs emotional outlets. If not found in personal relationships, this need can be relieved by artistic self-expression. In the case of Dwight, this expression took the form of musical composition. Despite possible emotional hurts when he was young, his interest in relatedness has served Reginald Kenneth Dwight well, for his professional association with Bernie Taupin has led to the composition of songs that effectively relate the feelings, frustrations, and needs of today's youth.

In looking at the component colors within his expression as Reginald Kenneth Dwight, we find blue dominant and indigo absent.

COLORS IN REGINALD KENNETH DWIGHT

red	orange	yellow	green	blue	indigo	violet	rose	gold
1	3	1	2	7	0	2	2	3

With blue accented within his orange expression, it is likely that Dwight roamed the gamut of contemporary music in search of his own individualized style. In fact, before effecting his own style he is known to have released songs that were based on the styles of other musical performers. As indigo is often related to the family, the absence of this function in his expression would seem to indicate possible fears, frustrations, or inhibitions in the youthful Dwight as a result of the family structure. While the lack of indigo may have given him an indrawn nature tending toward loneliness, the dominance of blue could have forced him to have greater faith in himself and eventually result in the aspirations to achieve, to expand beyond the conventions of his childhood conditions, and to seek greater freedom in his self-expression.

In the inner urge we learn Reginald Kenneth Dwight was motivated by the violet function.

```
REGINALD  KENNETH  DWIGHT
 5 9 1     5   5      9     = 34 = 7,
                                violet
```

With a violet inner urge Reginald Kenneth Dwight may have been prodded by the need to realize his dreams and visions. Totally absorbing itself in a subject, violet seeks the primal causes behind the effects and dissects a subject in order to analyze in minute detail the parts to the whole. Violet is committed to perfection, for it knows that it can bring to man great masterpieces of culture. With Dwight there seems to have been such an urge. His ambition to become a musician was resolute, despite his father's constant discouragement. Able to play the piano by ear at the age of four, Dwight later studied music at the Royal Academy of Music in London. When he was seventeen, he quit school and totally committed himself to becoming a professional musician. His ambitions were to be realized, and the youth culture of the '70s benefited as a result.

In the latent self of Reginald Kenneth Dwight we find the function of green.

REGINALD KENNETH DWIGHT
9 7 5 34 2 55 28 45 782=76=13=4,
green

When alone by himself, Reginald Kenneth Dwight may have spent his time listening to music, practicing his music, virtually absorbing music in order to nourish his growth. Determined and conscientious, green seeks a purpose in life. For Dwight his purpose was his commitment to music. As green gives order and form to life, one can appreciate the amount of time he may have spent composing songs as a youngster. Yet through his interest in music he may have found security. No matter how overwhelmed he may have felt by the outside world, he could seek comfort and relief in his music.

In looking at his birthdate we see Reginald Kenneth Dwight's, Elton John's destiny to revolve around the green function.

MARCH 25, 1947
3+2+5+1+9+4+7=31=4, green

Throughout life his environment would seem to be one of continual growth and development. Concerned with the construction of forms, his destiny may be one of creating a constant source of hope and renewal. Where difficulty could arise is in green's tendency to be affected by practical realities, to get stuck in a rut and fixed in the security of tradition. As he progresses through life, Elton John should watch for any inclination to express his musical genius in a repetitious format or structure. There is no doubt that his musical abilities border on the genius. The question is whether he will use these abilities to continue to grow and expand his musical expression or whether his horizons will narrow, thereby leading to a stultifying process of composing songs whose structures are readily accepted but rather tedious. However, this possible pitfall is quite unlikely. For in the name Elton John we have an expression of

133

blue, emphasizing the trend toward change, exploration, and involvement in the many facets of music.

ELTON JOHN

53265 1685 = 41 = 5, blue

In his change of expression from the orange to the blue function we find the dominant color within his previous expression now becomes his primary mode of expression. As a result, it could produce a liberation from childhood inhibitions and less concern with the way others respond to his behavior. The blue of expression seems to fit Elton John, for there are few performers who are as dynamic and free in their self-expression. As blue roams the four corners of the world, so too does Elton John travel widely in concert. When we consider the component colors to his present expression, we find blue and indigo emphasized while green, violet, and gold are lacking in expression.

COLORS IN ELTON JOHN

red	orange	yellow	green	blue	indigo	violet	rose	gold
1	1	1	0	3	2	0	1	0

By a change in name Elton John has incorporated the indigo energy, totally lacking in him as a child. Not only does indigo become a strong factor in his expression, but, as we will see momentarily, it becomes the function of his latent self. The deep love and philosophical attitude of indigo could serve as an inspiration to him in the composition of his songs. Although green is absent in his expression, green will always be a part of him as the function of his destiny. With the lack of violet and gold there could be less concentration in the creation of his songs. As some critics have already accused him of doing, he might neglect the intense commitment of violet or the radiance of gold's perfection and merely churn out songs that are easily under-

134

stood and readily accepted by his listening public. For with blue as his expression there is the liability of a restlessness which could revolt against the necessary application to refine and perfect each composition.

As Elton John, his inner urge has shifted from violet to the rose function.

$$\text{ELTON JOHN}$$
$$5 \quad 6 \quad 6 \quad = 17 = 8, \text{rose}$$

While he may have been motivated by dreams of achievement as a child, it seems Elton John has a need to actualize visions into concrete forms. In his working relationship with Bernie Taupin it is interesting to note that John waits for Taupin to write the lyrics and then composes a song to fit the lyrics. With a rose inner urge there is the ability to work with others, usually in the capacity of directing the efforts of others. With Elton John we can see this tendency both in his associations with Taupin and Kiki Dee and in his ownership of the record company Rocket Records. John likely has the support and admiration of his co-workers, for with a rose inner urge there is the ability to guide people to their optimum potential. Accomplishment becomes paramount, especially on a large-scale. His need to attain, however, should be balanced by adequate relaxation, for the drive of rose could become overbearing and eventually debilitating to his physical body. As rose understands the realities of life conditions, John may be motivated to compose songs dealing with the emotions and struggles in life that all young people must face in growing up. Compassionate and aware of his own past experiences, Elton John would seem intent on offering his listening public a music of hope, understanding, and love.

Elton John's latent self is the color indigo.

By himself Elton John would seem relaxed and hospitable to any who entered his world. Recognizing his concept of family to include all those to whom he felt attachment, the family and the home would gain greater importance for him. He might seek to incorporate beauty, peace, and harmony in his home environment. As indigo often wants to be of service to others, it is possible that Elton John could become a pillar of his society, interested in the welfare and concerns of its citizens.

Through our color-number analysis perhaps we have learned more about Elton John. If advice were to be given to him, it would be to focus upon the violet and gold energies, to concentrate on the expansion of his creative talents, and to avoid the security of routinely turning out songs which are appealing yet repetitious. For there can be no doubt that Elton John is one of the musical geniuses of the '70s.

If we were to imagine a real-life Cinderella story, we might think of the subject of our third study, Sophia Scicolone. Although Sophia Scicolone's childhood was surrounded by poverty and war, she was to develop into both a great actress and a truly beautiful lady. For Sophia Scicolone eventually became Sophia Loren, whose physical beauty has left men in awe and whose elegance has won her the respect of other women. Born September 20, 1934, Ms. Scicolone had to work hard in order to rise beyond her humble beginnings, but the determination necessary to do so can be seen in her natal expression, the function of red.

SOPHIA SCICOLONE
1 6 7 8 9 1   1 3 9 3 6 3 6 5 5 = 73 = 10 = 1, red

To survive in the neighborhood of her youth the self-assertion of red would seem necessary. With red's emphasis upon the physical, much of Sophia Scicolone's initial appeal may have resulted from the image of passion so often associated with the color. Indeed, while she was trying to establish her career as an actress, she worked as a model for the Italian magazines that portray melodramas in photographs. As red gives the energy and drive to push forward objectives no matter what the obstacles, Ms. Scicolone's ambitions were not to be restrained. By the age of twenty-four she had won an acting trophy at the Venice Film Festival.

Within her expression we find an emphasis upon red, yellow, and indigo colors, while orange and green are lacking.

COLORS IN SOPHIA SCICOLONE

red	orange	yellow	green	blue	indigo	violet	rose	gold
3	0	3	0	2	3	1	1	2

The influence of the red, yellow, and indigo colors would strengthen in her expression the physical energy, the mind, and the feeling toward the family. With the intellect of the yellow attuned, she would learn rapidly and interest herself in communications with others. Adding to this characteristic indigo's interest in helping others, one can understand why Ms. Scicolone initially trained to become a schoolteacher. The cheer and happiness of yellow, combined with red's assertiveness, might have made her better able to overcome her early limitations by focusing upon the possibilities of the future. Yellow could also refine the red expression. Indigo would increase the importance of the family in her expression, and for Ms. Scicolone her family was a great influence upon her ambitions. For it was her mother who insisted she enter a beauty contest at the age of fifteen. Seeking beauty in whatever conditions prevail, indigo may have given her a more philosophical attitude toward her childhood environment. As we will note shortly, not only was indigo a factor in her expression, but it was also the function of her inner urge.

Where the energies were lacking in her childhood expression were in the orange and green colors. Both of these colors represent different qualities of balance. Although without green she may have neglected a system or structure for the advancement of her aims, we will see later the green function of her latent self. With orange missing there might have been difficulty in balancing the physical energy and the intellect. As a result, she could have experienced trouble through her associations with others. Without orange and with red and yellow accented, Ms. Scicolone may have swung between the extremes of a passionate expression of anger, haste, and recklessness and a cold, dispassionate attitude, lacking in emotional warmth. Yet balance often allows indolence, and for Sophia Scicolone effort was necessary if she were to free herself from the poverty of her childhood.

As mentioned earlier, her inner urge vibrated to the indigo function.

$$S\ O\ P\ H\ I\ A\quad S\ C\ I\ C\ O\ L\ O\ N\ E$$
$$6\quad\ \ 9\ 1\quad\ \ \ 9\ \ 6\ \ 6\ \ 5 = 42 = 6, \text{indigo}$$

Indigo's recognition of the discrepancy between the reality of what is and the vision of what could be may have been a strong motivating factor for Sophia Scicolone in her efforts to be of service. Although born to a world of frustration and discord, Ms. Scicolone must have understood the beauty contained in all life. As we noted previously, the family played an important part in her initial expression. There would seem to have been an urge within her to realize the role of motherhood by which she could nourish others. Initially, this attitude took the form of an interest in teaching. Later, it was prominent in her earlier films where she often portrayed a wife confronted by problems. Eventually, this inner urge would find its expression through marriage to Carlo Ponti and in her children. Determined to

138

create beauty amidst the sordid environment man has devised for himself, indigo might have been the force necessary to interest Ms. Scicolone in the artistic by which she could express man's ability to rise above conditions and to create a world of beauty and love for himself. Indeed, Ms. Scicolone's life has been a vibrant expression of just such an ability.

In her latent self, we find the function of green which was lacking in her expression.

$$\text{SOPHIA SCICOLONE}$$
$$1 \quad 78 \quad \quad 13 \quad 3 \quad 3 \quad 5 \quad = 31 = 4, \text{ green}$$

By herself, Sophia Scicolone would seem influenced by green's concern with establishing peace, balance, and security to the life. Because of the fact that her childhood was spent in a less than peaceful environment, she may have felt restless and discontent but always desirous of attaining peace and harmony. If this were so, it could have catalyzed her to overcome her early conditions. For security is seen as a product of definite achievements, tangible forms. Patient and determined, green will expend whatever effort is necessary to realize its purpose. One can imagine the amount of time Ms. Scicolone devoted to refining her qualities and developing her potentials.

In her birthdate of September 20, 1934, we find her destiny to be of the red function.

$$\text{SEPTEMBER 20, 1934}$$
$$9+2+0+1+9+3+4 = 28 = 10 = 1, \text{ red}$$

Throughout her life, Sophia Scicolone, Sophia Loren will live in an environment similar to her expression as Sophia Scicolone. The need to assert herself, to express her individuality, to push forward her objectives, will always have the opportunity of realization.

By changing her name to Sophia Loren, Ms. Scicolone has incorporated her inner urge in both her expression and her latent self.

$$SOPHIA \ LOREN$$
$$167891 \ 36955 = 60 = 6, \text{indigo}$$

As Sophia Loren, her expression has become that of the indigo function. Her urge to serve others is now expressed both through her films and through her domestic life. Unlike some actresses who attain worldwide stardom, Ms. Loren has not been tarnished by the fantasized decadence of the world of the silver screen. On the contrary, much of her recent acclaim has resulted from her individual emphasis upon her children, her family, and her graciousness. Through her example she has offered women the respect deserving of womanhood. Unwilling to merely flaunt a virtually flawless physical beauty, Ms. Loren has expressed for all of us true beauty—the elegance of character, the beauty within.

Although sensationalists might accuse her expression of being a public relations sham, we see Ms. Loren's latent self vibrates to the indigo function. Her expression is no sham but is real.

$$SOPHIA \ LOREN$$
$$1 \ 78 \quad 3 \ 9 \quad 5 = 33 = 6, \text{indigo}$$

Alone she would seem intent upon her family and her children. To know that Sophia Scicolone has realized her inner urges perhaps adds to the fairy-tale quality of her life. But her achievement is to our benefit. For not only has she allowed us to see beauty and love grow from the midst of war and poverty, but she has made us recognize that each one of us can rise above our early life conditions and develop the potentials of our character.

COLORS IN SOPHIA LOREN

red	orange	yellow	green	blue	indigo	violet	rose	gold
2	0	1	0	2	2	1	1	2

Within her expression as Sophia Loren we find the energies of red, blue, indigo, and gold strongest, while the orange and green colors are absent. Her presentation to the world will still emphasize her individuality and the self-assertion of the red energy which is her destiny and her natal expression. Although blue may add to her tranquillity of bearing, it may also involve her in change, travel, and a multitude of activities. This tendency can be seen in the fact that during the early 1950s Ms. Loren was in over twenty films within the space of three years. Already we have seen the indigo function heavily accented in Sophia Loren as both her mode of expression and her latent self. The gold will color her expression with a radiance of the perfect beauty of her soul. As we will note momentarily, the gold function has now become her inner urge.

The deficient energies in her present expression are those functions lacking in Sophia Scicolone—the orange and the green colors. While Ms. Scicolone's latent self vibrated to the green function, neither green nor orange are represented in Sophia Loren. The difficulty in balancing her energies could be ever more apparent. If we were to counsel Ms. Loren on her energies as indicated through the color-number analysis, we would indicate the possible need to incorporate greater balance within her life structure. The spontaneity of red and the restlessness of blue could take charge of her expression. As a result, she might involve herself in activities without ordering her time or her commitments to participation. If she were not careful, such an attitude could lead to the dissipation of her energies and harm to her well-being.

As Sophia Loren, her inner urge is the gold function.

$$\begin{array}{cccc} \text{S O P H I A} & \text{L O R E N} \\ 6 \quad 9\,1 \quad 6 \quad 5 & =27=9, \text{gold} \end{array}$$

Motivated by the gold energies, Ms. Loren would seem influenced by the need to communicate the light of hope and cheer. Through her experience she has gained an understanding of the truth and love to be found in living. Within her radiates a warmth and vitality. And who can deny the nourishment Ms. Loren has given to the world? Whether we have marvelled at her physical beauty, whether we have admired her dauntless determination to transcend her early conditions, whether we have respected her devotion to her children and family, each one of us, touched by her life, has been affected. True to her inner urge, Ms. Loren expresses through the indigo function the motivation of the gold—to emanate like a sun the brilliancy of life's beauty. The intensity with which she lives her life offers each of us an inspiration. No matter how frustrating our lives are at times, we have no cause to complain. For, as shown by Ms. Loren's achievements, any one of us can decide to perfect our qualities and create for ourselves a life of beauty and harmony. We should all be grateful to Sophia Loren for her example.

The last person to be considered through our color-number analysis technique is a man who has established himself as a powerful and versatile actor. Few actors in their work have explored the range of characters or the depths of personality as has Jack Nicholson. Born April 22, 1937, Jack Nicholson's expression vibrates to the rose function.

$$\begin{array}{cc} \text{J A C K} & \text{N I C H O L S O N} \\ 1\,1\,3\,2 & 5\,9\,3\,8\,6\,3\,1\,6\,5=53=8, \text{rose} \end{array}$$

With a driving energy to construct material forms out of ideas rose will not spare itself. This attitude can be seen in Nicholson's efforts, for one need only think of his commitment in time and energy to the roles he has played. Prior to the filming of *One Flew over the Cuckoo's Nest*, Nicholson spent the time to understand the reality of being inside a mental institution. Rose understands human psychology, for it has experienced life and harbors few illusions about reality. In his film portrayals Nicholson has often played the antihero, the individual whose life is intertwined with frustrations, with confusions, with the reality of living. While some of his characters effect an image of impotent desperation, Nicholson plays them with such force and power as to give them a limited freedom of their individuality. As rose gives the scope of vision to see all the parts of a situation and the ability to integrate these parts into a working whole, Nicholson can not only act but could direct and guide the ideas for a film to their successful completion. In fact, Nicholson is not only a talented actor but has won acclaim for his writing and his directing. Rose expresses the need to achieve, and indeed, Jack Nicholson has achieved lasting recognition as one of the great actors in this contemporary period.

COLORS IN JACK NICHOLSON

red	orange	yellow	green	blue	indigo	violet	rose	gold
3	1	3	0	2	2	0	1	1

Within his expression Jack Nicholson has red and yellow emphasized, with green and violet absent. The red would give him the incentive to follow his own course, to create the means necessary for his own self-assertion. The individuality would be accented by a passionate need to experience life. The energy of red can be seen in the intensity of Nicholson's film portrayals, where he often depicts characters struggling to define their individuality amidst conditions of conformity. With yellow strong in his expression, there can be little doubt that Nicholson's mental faculties are well developed. Interested in ideas and in learning, Nicholson absorbs himself in the lives of his characters, investigating their whims and nuances of personality. As yellow seeks to communicate with others, acting would seem a natural for Jack Nicholson. A cheerful, pleasing color, yellow could imbue Nicholson with a sparkling, fun-loving personality that attracts many friends and admirers. But yellow needs variety and freedom. For Nicholson this attitude has found expression in his involvement both in the various functions of film-making and in the different characters he has played in recent years.

With the violet energy absent, the visions of a better world may seem mere fantasies. In his films to date Jack Nicholson has primarily portrayed individuals totally immersed in the practical realities of mundane conditions. The frustrations of their lives become ever more poignant when one realizes their lack of hope for a better future, except perhaps through escapes of desperation. This attitude is seen in Nicholson's role as George Hanson in *Easy Rider*, where Hanson, prior to joining Captain America and Billy in their travels, states, "This used to be a hell of a good country; I don't know what happened." The green energy absent in his expression would amplify the violet lack. Balance would be missing, and growth might be viewed as the result of conditions becoming so frustrating as to necessitate radical, even violent, change. Life would seem to hold no purpose. Routine and ordered structures could be scorned in favor of a wandering aimlessness. In several of his portrayals Jack Nicholson has expressed just such an attitude. However, although the green energy may seem deficient in his expression, we find the green function to be the color of both his inner urge and his latent self.

INNER URGE

$$1 \quad 9 \quad 6 \quad 6 \quad =22=4, \text{green}$$

J A C K N I C H O L S O N

$$1 \quad 32 \quad 5 \quad 38 \quad 31 \quad 5=31=4, \text{green}$$

LATENT SELF

With the green function as both the motivation factor of his inner urge and his latent self when alone by himself, we find in Jack Nicholson the need and the desire to develop his potentials. As indicated by his career, Nicholson is concerned with structure and order in his work. The determination and conscientiousness of green can be seen in the quality of his performances, which have won him not only several Academy Award nominations but eventually his first Oscar. His emphasis upon precision and his understanding of proportion not only allow him to portray characters of varying dimensions effectively but provide him with a strong aptitude in direction as well. For green's interest in creation would give Nicholson the ability to shape ideas into meaningful forms. Although he may seem to have a devil-may-care attitude, Nicholson is developing into one of the truly great craftsman in the film industry.

Born April 22, 1937, Jack Nicholson's destiny revolves around the red function.

APRIL 22, 1937

$$4+2+2+1+9+3+7=28=10=1, \text{red}$$

The environment of red would seem to always provide Nicholson with the opportunity to assert his individuality, to express himself. Activity and movement will occupy his life, for the expansive nature of red may continually involve him in seeking new channels for self-expression. Whether as actor, writer, or director, Nicholson has the ability to depict the experience of life through his work. One might hope, however, that Nicholson would ingrain more of the absent violet function in his work. For Nicholson's talents could pro-

145

vide the public not merely with the sense of frustration and desperation in present day's societal conditions but with a vision of improvement in life by the individual's willingness to struggle and persevere. As red is an initiator, a pioneer, a creator, Jack Nicholson can prove to be one of the most skillful yet revolutionary architects of the film industry.

By means of the color-number analysis technique we have explored the rainbows of four well-known personalities and have seen why they are who they are. Now how about yourself? Perhaps with your own color rainbow you can increase your state of self-awareness. For it is only through discovering our individual qualities of character that each of us can truly grow according to our own unique structure. With an understanding of ourselves and with our commitment to constantly improve our character, the frustrations in our lives can be alleviated. The first step toward self-improvement is the greater appreciation of our individuality. The second step is to correct our flaws and perfect our qualities. Once we are aware of who we are we have a starting point from which we can do both. And in our conscious application of color we have a tool to help us in our work. In the forthcoming section we will deal with various techniques to incorporate a greater consciousness of the colors in our lives.

Chapter 7

Color Breathing and Visualizations

Although we may have gained a greater appreciation and understanding of the influence of color in our lives through the last two sections, we must apply this knowledge in a conscious manner if we are to reap benefit from color. Having seen color as the refraction of white light into differentiated vibratory frequencies, we can recognize the distortion of reality practiced by today's society in its emphasis upon "sameness" and similarity. Perhaps through the different color rainbows we have devised for ourselves and our friends we are beginning to accept the fact that each one of us is a different blend of qualities, a varied pattern of energies. Consequently, we can more fully appreciate the term "identity," with its meaning of exact sameness in all respects, as the figment of superficial investigation.

As we delve ever further into the examination of any situation, any object, any individual, we draw out additional characteristics to differentiate each situation, each object, each individual. On a surface level, we can classify. On a multi-ordinal level, we must accept classification as both a variable and a restriction imposed upon the reality of the situation, object, or individual. The same is true in our lives.

By becoming overly narrow in our vision, we have imposed upon ourselves various restrictions to our growth and our development. We have assumed similarities and have seen differences as individual quirks. We seek conformity from others, as if in conformity there is security. But security can only be found in oneself. No matter how many external possessions we may have, no matter how many flattering compliments we may get, they mean nothing if we feel insecure within ourselves. And where does this insecurity come from? Generally speaking, it arises through the discrepancy between the reality of our individual being and the standards of our society which detail the accepted expectations of achievement.

Deep within ourselves in an unconscious, instinctual manner we do understand ourselves. But we are afraid to appear different, to be individual, to grow according to our own structure. And so we find some people frustrated by life, for such people have not allowed themselves the differences between all living forms. Yet here lies security—in the uniqueness of the individual being, in the diversity between peoples, in the sharing of another's experiences.

The purpose of the color rainbow is to make us more aware of our individual characteristics and thereby allow us the freedom of being ourselves. If we have gained insights into ourselves through the color rainbow, then it has served its purpose. But once we are aware of our qualities and characteristics, then the work begins. For now that we have begun to understand our lives as creative self-expressions different from another's work in the living art, we can alleviate the miseries we too often create for ourselves and can improve the quality of our lives.

In this chapter we will deal with three techniques to

increase our consciousness of color's reality and to use color as a means to self-development.

I. TECHNIQUE IN PERCEPTIVE AWARENESS

Our first technique intends for us to look at reality. In a sense, reality is experienced only when we heed the advice of Gautama Buddha to follow the middle path or, in essence, to have no opinions. To view life situations without our opinions, without our traditional values, without our prejudices indeed helps us to clean away the distortions to our perspective of reality.

When we allow ourselves to experience reality with preconceived anticipations and expectations, we devise for ourselves a fantasy world where reality is seen only from our subjective viewpoint. As our minds often run rampant with vague dreams, fears, hallucinations, we then live in our imaginings and lose the reality of experience to our mental conceptions. Any sensory stimulant seems to trigger our minds off on a yellow brick road of fantasy and delusion. In the accelerating process of our society we find ourselves constantly bombarded by stimulants. Our concentration has been shattered, and the quality of our lives has deteriorated as a result. Therefore, we must build anew our concentration. Through our first technique we will work at applied concentration in order to free ourselves from being held captive by our fictitious conceptions. In this technique and in any work upon one's self, recognize that each of us must take responsibility for our own individual actions and our own mental ramblings.

To begin our first technique, take your samples of the seven colors of Newton's spectrum: red—orange—yellow—green—blue—indigo—violet. As we realize rose and gold are the first two colors of the next octave of the color spectrum and are the higher frequencies correspondent to the red and orange colors, we will return our attention to the seven colors of Newton's spectrum in the three color breathing and visualization techniques explained in this chapter.

Put the red color swatch before you. Take several deep breaths and relax. Get comfortable. Now focus your attention on the red color swatch. Look at it without thinking of anything else. Check to see where your point of consciousness is. Does it wander away from the red swatch? When your concentration on red is interrupted, try to recall the mental concerns that stole your attention from the red color swatch. Where did your mental ramblings take you? Did you parade through associations of red-colored objects? Did you file through all the objects you mentally classify under "red"? Did you recall the various anxieties in your present-day living process? Did you wonder what someone else was doing? About other things you could be doing? Where did you go? Without guilt or anxiety, trace your steps back along the path of diversions from your concentration on the red swatch. Begin to realize the number of times you lose present reality to your mental ramblings.

Return your attention to the red swatch. Focus on the red swatch. As you do so, become aware of your life rhythms. Feel your breath . . . the flowing of energy into your body as you inhale . . . the eliminating of toxins from your body as you exhale. Once your point of consciousness becomes cognizant of the pulsation of your living process and more aware of your inner self, extend your consciousness out to a red-colored object. Experience the red object. Perceive the object without your mental definitions of the object. Sense the effect the object has upon you. How does it make you feel?

Do you have difficulty concentrating on the object? Initially, you probably do. Return your concentration to your organic processes. Take a few deep breaths. Relax. In the inhalation and exhalation of the life force in the air feel flowing through you the process of life, the process representative of the tidal systems in man's being.*

When you regain your awareness of your inner self, let your consciousness reach out again to the red object. Can you see yourself and the object as two different energy patterns? How do you relate to the red object? Does it excite you? Does it antagonize you? What is your reaction to the red object? What is your experience of that object?

After you have explored the red object and the red color, move to the next color of Newton's spectrum, orange. Take the orange color swatch and focus your attention on it. Follow the same procedure you followed for the red color. When you see your attention wandering from the orange color swatch, take a moment to reflect on where your mind was roaming. Then return your attention to the orange color and experience it without your likes or dislikes, without your opinions, without your anxieties distorting the reality of experience. Although concentration on the orange swatch may be difficult at first, become more aware of your breathing as you look at the orange swatch. Still looking at the orange swatch, take several deep breaths, relax, and sense the process of breathing in your body. Feel your body fill with life force as you breathe in. Feel your body empty of tensions as you breathe out. Once you have reawakened your sense of the inner self, extend your consciousness out to an orange-colored object.

How does the orange-colored object affect you? Does it enliven you? Does it make you timid? What is your response to the vibratory rapport established through the contact point of energy patterns between yourself and the object? What is your experience of the orange object and the color orange?

Continue this process of concentration for the other five colors of Newton's spectrum. Initially, focus on the color swatch. Become alert to your mental diversions from concentration. See where they lead you. Then seek to align yourself to your natural processes of life. Relax; take several deep breaths. Become aware of your breathing process with its phases of inhalation and exhalation. Return your attention to the color. As you become more cognizant of your inner life, extend your consciousness out to an object which is the color of the swatch focused upon. Experience the object. How does the object affect you? If you find your concentration failing you, return to a focusing upon your breathing. Once you have calmed the mental turmoil, return your attention again to the object. Perceive the object without your definitions. Sense your reaction to the object and the color.

After you have concentrated on yellow and seen your reaction to that color, move on to green. Then blue, indigo, violet. Experience each of the seven colors and see how each one affects your emotional attitude. No time limit for the exercise is necessary. Do the technique in a manner that is comfortable for you. But perform it in a synchronized manner. Go through the spectrum in order, from red through violet. While the red end of the spectrum has the longest wavelengths of color, violet has the shortest wavelengths at the more vibratory end of the spectrum. Through the orderly progression of the color spectrum, recognize each color as an individualized pattern of energy and sense the effect of each color upon you.

II. CONSCIOUS IMAGINATION TECHNIQUE

Often when we feel tired, we can retrace part of the cause to our permitting ourselves to go on automatic control. Neglecting conscious awareness, we become led by our habits, our opinions, our emotions. Much of our life energy drains from us as a consequence of our mental ramblings in similarities and associations. We allow our imaginations to run riot. And yet it is through the functional use of the mind that we gain rational control of our own lives. In the Conscious Imagination Technique we take control of our imagination and direct it toward the absorption of the life energies in colors with their correspondent effects upon our level of mental consciousness.

Before starting this technique, relax, take several deep breaths, get comfortable.

With this tool we are able to scale the heights in man's attempts to align himself to life's rhythmic patterns of order. Through the use of our mind we will climb a mountain of the spectrum of color. Starting from our base camp of red, there are seven levels where reality is filtered through one of the seven colors of the spectrum. Upon reaching each level, we will halt our climb in order to experience the reality of that level.

If you will be aware that any journey is taken one step at a time, the climb will not be an arduous one. Throughout the ascent, be conscious of your breathing. Close your eyes and focus upon your breathing. Seek to establish a natural, comfortable rhythm to your breathing. See before you a mountain of color.

We are at the base camp. We see our base camp through a red filter. Everything we see is red. The flowers, the shrubs, our crude rough lodging . . . everything is colored red. We feel great excitement, for we are readying ourselves to climb a mountain whose summit looms largest at its base. But we are confident, for we can do it. We breathe in deeply to steel our fortitude. We feel our red blood coursing through our veins. We are alive, truly alive. Our bodies tingle with physical vitality.

Breathe in the red with each inhalation. As you continue to breathe in red, feel your energy level pick up. Feel your fears in life drop away, as the red energy pours into your body the courage to be yourself. Use your imagination to color in red your mental visions of the base camp scene. Everything you see, color in red. Experience the red level.

We are now prepared. We have vitalized our bodies through the excitement and stimulus of the red energy. It is time to forge upward from our base camp to the second level.

As we reach our second level, we see everything colored in orange. We feel cheered, for our initial fears of climbing have passed. From our experience gained in our ascent from the base camp to the second level of orange, we have begun to understand the reality of mountain climbing. Recognizing the need to temper our expenditures of energy, we are now more aware of the importance of balance.

Breathe in the orange with each inhalation. As you continue to breathe in the orange, feel your body fill with the joy of accomplishment. Feel your inhibitions drop away, as you become more aware of both your physical vitality and your mental powers. Use your imagination to color in orange your mental visions of this second level. Everything you see from this level is colored in orange. Experience the orange plateau.

From our orange plateau we climb to our next level where reality is filtered through the color yellow. Although we feel more optimistic, we are not as emotionally excited as before. Our reasoning faculties restrain the tendency to impulsiveness. Our minds become filled with mental stirrings and ideas. We recognize the power of the mind and intend to use it consciously.

Breathe in the yellow with each inhalation. As you continue to breathe in the yellow, feel your mind expanding. No longer driven by instinct, you have the opportunity to use your mental faculties to guide your behavior. Sense the freedom to be gained through the functional use of the mind. As if rising above cloud cover, feel the life force of yellow saturate your body with happiness and a zest for living. Use your imagination to color in yellow your mental visions of this third level. Everything you see from this level is colored in yellow. Experience the yellow plateau.

From yellow we climb to the green level, where we

reach the halfway mark in our ascent through the spectrum of color. We rest in the tranquillity of our green surroundings. Aware of the importance of system and order to our efforts, we alternate activity with rest. Patient yet determined in our endeavors, we feel more at peace within ourselves.

Breathe in the green with each inhalation. As you continue to breathe in the green, feel a greater balance within yourself. Feel the life force of green soothe your taut muscles and relax your entire body. Sense the harmony achieved between your physical, outer nature and your spiritual, inner nature, as you resolve to structure your activities through the conscious use of your mind. Use your imagination to color in green your mental visions of this level. Everything you see from this level is colored in green. Experience the green plateau.

From our halfway mark at green we climb to the blue plateau. Before us extends eternity, for our sight is freed from the limitations imposed by a valley perspective. We feel the intensity to the depth of life. The endless process of living stretches out to us in the vistas of the heavens and the earth. We feel more secure in the reality of the eternal.

Breathe in the blue. As you continue to breathe in the blue, feel greater faith in your being an integral and essential factor to life's present reality. Let the life force of blue relieve you of the anxieties you have devised from a lack of true understanding. Feel the blue instigate curiosity as a motivation for you to progress ever onward and experience the reality of life's endless process. Use your imagination to color in blue your mental visions of this level. Everything you see from this level is colored in blue. Experience the blue plateau.

From the blue plateau we climb to the indigo level. From where we stand, our awareness of the process of life seems heightened, for the complications in our living seem like fantasies. We recognize our daily lives to be the programs of our own creation. Not distorted by our mundane conditions, our perception of reality is clearer and our intuitive understanding increased.

Breathe in the indigo with each inhalation. As you continue to breathe in the indigo, feel the diverse parts of your nature being aligned into a harmonious, working whole. Sense the discrepancy between the reality of life and the way you live it. Let the life force of indigo fill your body with the warmth of love. Feel in indigo the ability to adapt to changing situations with an understanding of life's relativity. Use your imagination to color in indigo your mental visions of this level. Everything you see from this level is colored in indigo. Experience the indigo plateau.

From the indigo level we climb and reach the summit of our color mountain at the violet plateau. Behind us lies the known, before us the unknown. We face the future without fears, for we recognize these preconceptions to be fictions erased only by experience. From our experiences we have gained an appreciation of the reality behind the appearances. We are inspired by the unfolding of reality.

Breathe in the violet with each inhalation. As you continue to breathe in the violet, feel yourself inspired to delve beyond surface appearance into reality, into the truth. Let the life force of violet fill you with dreams of perfection. Feel the violet strengthen your resolve to develop your qualities of being, to correct your flaws of character, and to reflect constantly upon your life experiences, as if each one were a subject of study. Use your imagination to color in violet your mental visions of this level. Everything you see from this level is colored in violet. Experience the violet plateau.

Through this technique of consciously controlling the imaginative faculties of the mind we have experienced the seven colors of the spectrum and their correspondent energy frequencies. With this stimulus of color we have absorbed into our bodies the differentiated life energies fundamental to our healthy functioning.

The Conscious Imagination Technique can and should be modified to fit your individual needs. But the importance of the technique cannot be overstated. Not only does it allow for a focusing on the breathing process, but it offers a method to work consciously with the imagination.

III. TECHNIQUE IN ENERGY ABSORPTION

In our third technique of color breathing and visualization we move toward a greater use of the mind. Initially, with the Technique in Perceptive Awareness, we concentrated on the colors through our reliance upon the physical stimulants of color swatches and colored objects. Our purpose in that technique was both to gauge our reaction to the different colors and to work with our focused attention. In the second technique, the Conscious Imagination Technique, we worked with the imaginative faculties of the mind through our imagining participation in a climb up a mountain of color. By using our imagination in a functional, concentrated application, we experienced the seven colors. In our third technique we progress further with the use of our imagination and breathing to absorb the varied energies of the color spectrum into our bodies. Prior to working this exercise, it might be wise to re-familiarize ourselves with the characteristics of each color. Therefore, consider re-reading Chapter IV in order to understand more thoroughly the characteristics of each of the seven colors.

Before you start the technique, relax and begin to focus your attention upon your breathing. Sit comfortably and close your eyes. Sense your alignment to the natural order through the realization that our organic processes are similar and correlative to the organic processes happening in nature.

Focus upon your breathing. Feel yourself inhaling the life energies of the universe as you breathe in and exhaling the anxieties, fears, and frustrations within you as you breathe out. Seek a comfortable and natural rhythm to your breathing. Eliminate all thoughts. Your attention should be totally focused upon the process of breathing. Once you have gained control of your mind and feel yourself comforted by the rhythmic life force of your body's breathing, begin this Technique in Energy Absorption.

As you sit comfortably with your eyes closed and your attention focused upon your breathing, visualize an orb of red energy hovering above your head. As you breathe in, imagine the red energy of this orb being inhaled into your body. Breathe deeply, but comfortably. In the inhalation feel your body absorb the red energy. Feel the red enter your lungs and expand into your legs, your arms, your head. Feel yourself as porous, with the red energy flowing through every pore of your body. As you exhale, feel the toxins of your worries, concerns, and pains being eliminated from your body. Breathe in the red energy seven times.

After the seventh rhythmic inhalation of the red energy, visualize an orb of orange energy hovering above your head. Breathe in the orange energy seven times. As you inhale, feel the orange color flowing throughout your body. As you exhale, feel your anxieties being flushed away. After the seventh time of breathing in the orange energy, breathe in the yellow energy seven times. After yellow, follow this process of inhalation-exhalation through the color spectrum with green, blue, indigo, and violet. As you breathe in, feel your body glow with the color you are absorbing. Feel the qualities of that color fill every part of your being. On each exhalation feel your body expel the poisons of your living patterns. Breathe each color seven times in the full cycle of inhalation-exhalation. After you have finished breathing in the spectrum of color with the last color violet, continue your rhythmic breathing.

As you breathe in, visualize an orb of white light hovering above your head. Breathe in the white light.

Feel the white light cleanse and purify your entire being. On each exhalation feel the white light break up energy blockages in your body and clear them from your being. Breathe in the white light seven times.

After you have finished the technique, rest. Mentally record your reactions to the technique. What was your experience with this technique? Did it calm you? Did it vitalize you? How do you feel after working the technique?

We now have three color breathing and visualization techniques by which we can absorb the life energies that are constantly around us. With these tools we can work upon ourselves. Although our society fosters the expectation of instant results, we will get out of these techniques only as much as we are willing to put in. But through the conscious application of life energies we can correct our unhealthy living patterns. We can improve the quality of our lives. No longer need we be locked into misery or frustration by our incorrect habits of living. We can begin to develop our lives daily. Yet each of us has the responsibility for our own well-being. No one else can make us better our lives. Only we can. The choice is up to each one of us. For those who choose to work with color as such a means of absorbing life energies, the next chapter will offer various insights into the conscious use of color to coordinate our everyday lives.

Chapter 8

Color Hints

In Chapter VII we learned three techniques by which to absorb into our bodies the differentiated energies of the color spectrum. In this present chapter we will discuss various means to incorporate color in our daily lives. By now probably each of us has devised our own color rainbow through the color-number technique. From our individual rainbows we have become aware of the colors of our being, of the colors dominant and the colors lacking within ourselves. As we have gained a greater appreciation for and understanding of the significance of color, it is time that we acknowledge ourselves to be the artists of our lives. If we are willing to take responsibility for our patterns of living, each of us can become a genius in the art of life. We can regain the paradise lost and create for ourselves truly beautiful lives. By using color consciously in our everyday activities, we can turn our lives around. We can enjoy life instead of being frustrated by it.

This chapter offers suggestions for the use of color

in our homes, in our wardrobes, in our food selection, and for our health. Recognize that these are merely suggestions. Throughout this book the emphasis has been upon differentiation and individuality. We have stressed differences between one another in contrast to the mythical belief in identity of one another. The color hints given must be general in outlook. They give us an idea as to the *general* effect of colors, according to the color characteristics and their energy levels. Some of the suggestions offered may not be relevant to our specific life patterns, to our own energy levels. But the validity of these color hints to our lifestyles is dependent upon our use of them and our experience with them. With these suggestions, modified by our own experiences and understanding, we can color our everyday lives with a plethora of energies helpful to the improvement of our well-being. Such is the purpose of this chapter—to relate color to its conscious application in our daily lives.

COLOR IN THE HOME

When we first described the characteristics of color, we stated that the red end of the spectrum with its longer wavelengths was more physically oriented while the violet end of the spectrum with its shorter wavelengths was more spiritually oriented. Red, orange, and yellow are warm, exciting, and stimulating colors. Violet, indigo, and blue are cool, relaxing, and calming colors. In the use of color to decorate our homes we should be aware of the red end of the spectrum as being more aggressive in its effects. These colors seem to advance toward us and concentrate our attention. The violet end of the spectrum is softer. These colors seem to retreat from us and provide a spaciousness. Consequently, the violet, indigo, and blue colors are more appropriate for background use and the red, orange, and yellow for highlights.

In discussing the individual colors for various uses within our homes, red would be beneficial for those areas of the house devoted to physical exercise. Red could be used in playrooms, for it fosters excitement, high spirits, and physical activity. While a red environment enhances the vitality, it also increases the passions. Red should be avoided where excitement could prove detrimental. Dining rooms accented with red can lead to a constant case of indigestion, resulting either from the bickering over the dinner table or from gulping down one's meal. While red in bedrooms might make a person feel passionate, it could also produce restlessness and insomnia. Red can be useful for the active areas of the house but not for areas designed for relaxation or concentration.

Orange would add to a room both the physical vitality of the red and the intellectual vivacity of the yellow. But orange would provide more of a mellow warmth to the room than would the raw, sometimes coarse, vitality of the red or the crisp, sometimes acerbic, intellect of the yellow. As orange accentuates an interest in associations and relationships, it could be used successfully in communal areas, rooms where you entertain friends or where the family gathers. Orange might also be beneficial for areas of study, for it gives energy and creative spontaneity to the mind. Although orange serves to highlight features in a room; used to excess, orange can feel overbearing in its self-indulgence.

Yellow provides a stimulus to the intellect and, therefore, should be considered for areas of the house where mental or creative interests are involved. Libraries and study rooms would benefit from the use of yellow. But for greater concentration, it might be wise to incorporate some green or violet to the room in order to balance off yellow's restlessness, engendered by the tendency toward a variety of interests. Yellow could be used anywhere in the house to add joy and happiness to the area. As yellow provides an impetus to keep conversations lively, it might be helpful in rooms where you entertain friends casually.

As green is a serene, peaceful color, it can prove useful in areas devoted to rest and relaxation. Bedrooms benefit from green, for it soothes the tensions in the body and calms the mind. Green supplies the energy of nourishment and natural growth. There can be no doubt that green coloring the kitchen would focus more energy on creativity in food preparation. But green should be kept to a minimum in rooms designed for advanced forms of creative self-expression, for it does tend to limit one to precedent and the status quo. Green might be wise in a man's workshop, where he is working with both his hands and his mind to translate his ideas into forms. Red, however, should be avoided in a workroom, for red's spontaneity and impulsiveness could result in careless accidents.

Blue lends a tranquillity to its surroundings and like green can be beneficial for rooms intended for relaxation and rest. Blue can be used in bedrooms, in dens, or in any rooms, which are small in size, to enlarge the feeling of space. For while green is more concrete, being related to the earthiness of nature, blue is more expansive, being associated with the spaciousness of infinity. If we have areas in the house were we go to reflect upon our life's experiences, where we can be alone with our thoughts, it might prove helpful to include in the coloring of the room any of the three colors, blue, indigo, violet.

When we discussed man's sense faculties and indicated the eventual development of two other senses along with the five functional at present, we mentioned that indigo and violet were seldom used in our color schemes. While this is true, it does not necessitate total elimination of these two colors from our home decoration. As we have seen throughout the book, color is merely differentiated energies. Although we may not actively respond to the higher frequencies of energy at this point in man's development, such a reality does not negate either the validity of, or the benefit from, the use of these colors. Therefore, if we are to absorb their representative life energies, we should consider inclusion of indigo and violet in coloring our homes.

Indigo encourages intuition, an innate understanding based on perception as opposed to concrete knowledge. Indigo could be used successfully in areas designed for introspection and creative work. Providing the stimulus to adjust problems to a harmonious resolution with justice and fairness, indigo may be beneficial in rooms where family situations are discussed and dealt with. As it nurtures the love in all relationships, indigo can color family rooms or casual rooms where friends gather. Let us recognize, however, that for most of us indigo is not as familiar a color as the earlier five colors discussed. We should use it sparingly, for too much of the indigo energy might lead to withdrawal and isolation from others.

Violet cultivates the tendency to accept nothing at face value, for true knowledge becomes the purpose under violet coloring. Violet may prove helpful in libraries or study rooms where applied concentration is needed. As it inspires the mind with dreams and visions, violet can be used in areas devoted to creative self-expression or in playrooms for young children to develop their imaginative faculties. Too much violet in a room might lead to escape from reality into a fantasy world. It would not be advised for those rooms where friends are entertained, for it could hinder the conversation and promote indulgence in drink or drugs. As mentioned previously, blue, indigo, and violet would be beneficial in rooms designed for introspection, reflection, and meditation.

Now that we have seen how color can be used functionally in the decoration of our homes, let us consider the use of color in illuminating our wardrobes.

COLOR IN THE WARDROBE

In our wardrobe it is often beneficial to use colors that have a special meaning for us. From our color rainbows we have found the colors that indicate our individual expression, inner urge, latent self, and destiny. By working with these colors in our clothing, we accentuate the different characteristics of our being. If we are going to a social function, we can highlight our apparel with the color of our expression. If we are at home by ourselves relaxing, we could wear the color of our latent self. If we feel the need for stimulus or motivation, we might adorn ourselves with the color of our inner urge or destiny. As well, we have realized the importance of balance. Through the color rainbows we have seen what energies are deficient within us as represented by the colors lacking in our rainbow. Dependent upon our purpose, we should incorporate our awareness of color in the selection of our wardrobe. If we use colors consciously in our dress, we may notice quite an effect upon both our attitude and our reception. Recognizing this approach to color to be an individualistic choice, let us briefly outline the possible effects of various colors in our wardrobe.

With red we project a passionate image with an air of vitality. Although red energizes, the energy often allows for extremes in behavior. Coloring our wardrobe with red can paint us with a spirit of independence and individuality or with a disposition toward aggression and argumentativeness.

With orange we project cheerfulness and an interest in others. We seem conscientious and considerate. If we properly coordinate our other accessories, we can depict ourselves as having an attuned sense of relationship and esthetic form. With too much orange, we might appear timid and dependent upon others.

With yellow we project a joy of living. Yellow colors us with an optimism and self-expression that appeals to others. Like the spreading of sunshine, yellow accents the charm of our personality. Although we might present an image of mental interest, yellow could also make us seem restless and over-extended in our activities.

With green we project an image of stability, tradition, and practicality. When we wear green, we seem more down to earth. While green might present us as efficient and determined, it could also make us appear rigid in our outlook. We may look well able to analyze but too narrow in vision for original thoughts.

With blue we project versatility with tranquillity. We appear competent to handle any situation. Wearing blue, we seem interested in change, freedom, and progress. As blue is an expansive color, too much blue could present us as totally committed to the freedom urge and unwilling to be restricted by the conventions of adopted standards.

With indigo we project an image of the unconventional. Primarily because of its limited use at present, indigo may be seen by some as being too impractical, individualistic, or radical. To others indigo might make us appear concerned with the welfare of others and interested in new ideas regarding philosophical and universal concepts.

With violet we project an image of the unconventional, yet inspired with the striving for the ideal. To some, violet might color us as a loner, a mystic, a dreamer divorced from mundane reality. But to those open to the energies of color, violet can present us as aware of life's opportunities and challenges and awaiting them without fear.

Having consciously colored our wardrobes, we will turn to the use of color in our food selection, where we will learn that we are what we eat.

COLOR IN THE FOOD

As we have discussed repeatedly, life is energy. Color, being the result of refracted white light, is merely one representation of the differentiation of energy patterns. But we no longer doubt the correlation between our own life forces and those of other energy patterns. Through the color rainbow we have learned more about ourselves and about others. Through our various insights from the study of color, through the functional techniques to use color consciously, we are able to work upon the conditions of our environment and thereby improve the state of our being. We now have come to another area where color can play a significant role. In our food selection we can plan our meals by choosing those foods whose colors are correspondent to the energies we feel we need.

For, in truth, we are what we eat. Our food is intended to nourish our bodies. In the digestion of food, our organic functions transform the food into energy and eliminate the wastes involved in the process of assimilation. But in our food selection we too often do not allow ourselves the time to pick our nourishment wisely. We clutter our kitchen cabinets with the things that appeal to our wants rather than those foods that are beneficial to our bodies. Yet how many of us have ever wandered into a bookstore to browse and found ourselves eventually looking at the pictures in the cookbooks of European kitchens? Those of us who have can admit to standing awed and in salivation over the color reproductions of various collages of elegant cuisine. While the pictures offer homage to masterpieces in food preparation, we can do the same. With our increased understanding of color, we can become both master chefs and master artists in the creation of our daily meals. No matter how simple the ingredients, our meals can become nourishing and festive with color.

For instance, we have all heard the suggestion of having a good breakfast to start off the day. But what is a good breakfast? Most of us are content with a slice of toast or a bowl of packaged cereal and a cup of coffee. Yet if we use our color awareness, we can derive from our breakfast the energy and vitality needed for the day ahead. By eating foods related to red, orange, and yellow, we can increase our energy level. Would it surprise you that many of us do make such a selection subconsciously? Those who drink orange juice for breakfast take in the orange energy. With coffee and eggs we take in the yellow energy. And if we have tomato juice or ketchup with our breakfast, we are taking in the red energy. However, if we understand this process of food selection, we can choose our food according to our energy needs and more consciously absorb the energies in the food.

At the evening meal, greens, such as a salad or green vegetable, would soothe our nerves and help us balance off the energy of the active day in preparation for a restful night. With a full quota of rest at night we re-charge our batteries and awaken refreshed and renewed the next day. We can see how coffee keeps many people awake. As coffee is related to the yellow energy, it operates as a stimulant.

During our development we have often been told subtle truths in clichés. If we are dragging and feel constantly tired, people suggest we need more "good red meat." Or if we tied one on the night before, we sometimes resort to a bloody Mary in the morning. Those more timid the morning after often substitute orange juice or a Virgin Mary of pure tomato juice to animate themselves. We all remember Popeye with his can of spinach which would transform him from inertia to intensity. For spinach combines the green energy of determination with the iron content related to red and red's energy of vitality. Those of us who hated carrots easily recall the constant and incessant pleadings for us to eat our carrots. Told they were good for our eyesight, we would resentfully eat the carrots with their orange energy.

Through the conscious application of color to our food selection, we can choose the energies we need to nourish our bodies and can establish a more balanced being within ourselves. From now on we can enter our grocery stores with a greater appreciation of food. For we may see before us the elements with which we can build our temple of life. Already, with our increased knowledge of color, we can gauge which colors to include in our meals. Generally speaking, the color of the skin of the fruits and vegetables often indicates the color energies those foods will provide our bodies. As we might expect, most of the foods we eat at present are related to the physical end of the spectrum, to the reds, oranges, yellows, and greens. To become aware of the correlation between foods and their colors, a partial listing is given below as a guide to help us see the relationship between foods and their colors.

RED:

apples	cloves	spinach
beets	red currants	strawberries
red cabbage	red plums	tomatoes
cayenne pepper	radishes	watercress
cherries	raspberries	

ORANGE:

apricots	oranges	rutabagas
cantaloupes	persimmons	saffron
carrots	pumpkins	tangerines
mangoes	nectarines	

YELLOW:

bananas	lemons	yellow peppers
coffee	honey-dew melons	pineapple
corn	mustard	prunes
eggs	olive oil	rhubarb
figs	parsnips	yellow squash
grapefruit	peaches	yams

GREEN:

avocado	vegetable greens	peas
beans	lettuce	green peppers
broccoli	okra	spinach
cucumber	olives	zucchini

BLUE:

blueberries	grapes	blue plums

INDIGO:
partakes of those foods under blue and violet

VIOLET:

blackberries	eggplant	purple grapes

COLOR IN HEALTH

Often when we take ill, our sickness is largely a result of the lack of balance in our living patterns. We overrun our physical vehicles or torment them with endless fictional worries and fears of anticipation. Our energy level suffers, and our bodies become highly susceptible to disease. If we decide to be the masters of our destiny as opposed to the customary followers of fate, we have various means to improve our state of being. This book has been dedicated to one of these means— the conscious use of energy patterns manifesting as colors. We have seen the benefit to be gained in the use of color. Perhaps we have even experienced it.

One area where color would seem to be helpful is in maintaining optimum health. We have learned color breathing and visualization techniques. We have increased our awareness of ourselves through the color rainbows. We have seen our choice of colors in relation to our homes, our clothes, our food. It is merely one step further to assume that color's effects upon us can not only change our attitudes and nourish our bodies but can alleviate some of the physical miseries caused

171

by our present lack of balance. Perhaps color can provide a remedy to our illnesses.

Although there are color institutes in England where color is recognized as an esoteric form of healing, color is not considered a valid method of cure in the United States. When we are sick or hurt, we should seek professional care. A doctor has the tools and techniques with which to diagnose our illness. Any esoteric forms of healing demand the complete faith of the patient. As the author does not claim substantive knowledge regarding the question of the effectiveness of color in curing sickness, he does not place his total faith in color healing. Although aware of the value of color in its conscious application to improve our daily lives, the author does not intend this section to be either a suggestion or affirmation of the use of color to cure illness. Rather, this section is a compendium of alleged remedies by treatment with color. For those readers interested in pursuing this realm of study, the bibliography provides reference works. Let it be known, however, that in the modern era color study and the use of color in healing dates from the late 1870s. Published records of cases do indicate the success in remedy of sickness through the use of color.

Red is a vitalizing, enlivening energy which stimulates the physical body and the nervous system. Its use has been recommended for:
* inertia, physical exhaustion
* the circulation of the blood, to raise blood pressure and pulse rate
* worry, fear
* colds, chills
* malnutrition, anemia, emaciation
* deficient menstruation

Stimulating both the physical vitality and the mental attitude, orange enlivens the emotions and produces a feeling of well-being. Its use has been recommended for:
* mental catatonia or infirmity
* the lungs, bronchitis, asthma

172

* emotional strains
* muscle spasm and cramps
* the kidneys
* hemorrhoids

Yellow radiates an optimistic, joyous energy which affects the nervous system and stimulates the mind. Its use has been recommended for:
* depression and mental lethargy
* stomach trouble, indigestion
* constipation, the bowels
* hard of hearing
* the skin
* the liver

Green's energy is a natural builder-upper, for it both relaxes the body by cooling the blood and refreshes the body by stimulating the nerves. Its use has been recommended for:
* high blood pressure, ulcers
* headaches
* sleeplessness
* nervous irritability or disorders
* boils
* muscle tension

Blue's energy of hope and serenity has a pacifying effect on the nervous system and mental attitude. Its use has been recommended for:
* sore eyes and earaches
* sore throat, laryngitis, hoarseness
* inflammations, infectious diseases
* nausea, diarrhea, gastritis
* excessive menstruation
* skin abrasions, cuts, burns, stings, itchings

Indigo's intuitive faculty provides the energy to relieve man's consciousness of fears, frustrations, and inhibitions. Its use has been recommended for:
* anesthesia, pain-killers
* the eyes, ears, nose, and throat
* lungs, pneumonia
* fevers

* skin diseases
* mental excitability, obsession

Violet's energy purifies the blood, calms the nerves, and inspires the brain to mental and spiritual uplift. Its use has been recommended for:

* neuralgia, sciatica
* diseases of the scalp, dandruff
* kidney and bladder ailments
* rheumatism
* neurosis, mental disorders
* insomnia

Chapter 9

The End of the Rainbow

We have now come to the end of our journey over the rainbow of color and color-consciousness. As legend would have us believe, we have discovered for ourselves a pot of gold. The pot of gold we have found, however, is not the gold of coins or material enrichment but rather the gold of the medieval alchemists. For through our travels we have found a tool, a means with which to turn the base metal of our inborn instincts and passions into the gold of awareness and coordinated living patterns. Before we bid adieu to one another, let us recount our journey.

Each of us came to this journey with our own ideas about color. After all, we had experienced color. We had seen it in the changing of the seasons. We had watched it in kaleidoscopic form turn a late afternoon into twilight with ever-changing color gradations. We had witnessed the sun, as it rose above the horizon in the east, paint the day with color. In our art museums we had viewed the color renderings of different personalities. We had clothed ourselves and decorated our homes in the colors we preferred. But how many of us knew what color was? How many of us recognized the importance of color to our lives? How many of us had truly experienced color? Perhaps too few. Too often in the past we had reacted to color without being aware of its significance to our lives.

At the beginning of our travels we explored the scientific reasons for color. We asked ourselves: What is color? What makes an object a certain color? We learned that at one time color was considered an inherent quality of an object. Until Isaac Newton revolutionized man's understanding of color, it was believed that an object contained color. In his work Newton discovered color to be the result of light falling upon an object and not an inherent attribute of the object. Newton proved this fact through his experiment of passing a beam of sunlight through a glass prism. As it passed through the prism, the beam of sunlight broke down into seven rays of colored light. Newton had classified the seven-tiered spectrum of color with its components of red, orange, yellow, green, blue, indigo, and violet. Not only had Newton established the seven-tiered spectrum of color, but in the second phase of his experiment he laid to rest the classical belief that color was an intrinsic part of an object. For after Newton had passed the beam of sunlight through the glass prism, he passed the seven differentiated color rays through a second prism. If the classical belief in color as a fundamental component of an object were true, Newton recognized that passing the differentiated rays through a second prism should lead to a further breaking down of the color rays. Such a result did not occur. Instead, the colors, upon emerging from the second prism, recomposed into a single beam of light.

From this basic understanding of color being the effect of the refraction of light, we questioned why an object is perceived as a certain color. Through the phenomenon of absorption and reflection we learned that when light falls upon an object, some of the color rays are absorbed within the object while others are reflected out. An object appears the color of those rays reflected out. Recognizing color to be an effect of light, we considered the theories related to light transmission and travel. Newton had proposed one theory which believed light to be a "thing" made up of minute material particles projected through space in a straight line. At virtually the same time as Newton described his Corpuscular Theory, Christiaan Huygens proposed the forerunner to the Wave Theory which believed light to be a "process" of disturbance of the atmosphere, acting like the ocean waves with their crests and troughs. With the turn of the twentieth century these two conflicting theories were both given their due validity when Max Planck introduced the atom into the concept of energy. Although the Wave Theory had gained dominance over Newton's theory, the Corpuscular Theory was revived by the experiments of Planck and Einstein. Yet neither of these scientists could explain away the phenomena of diffraction and interference to light which had gained support for the Wave Theory. As we ended our study of the scientific exploration of color, we realized that light has dual aspects. At times light behaves like a wave and at other times like a particle. At present we maintain this complementary relationship of light as both wave and particle.

To point out man's knowledge as being limited by his present conceptions and to counter twentieth-century man's vanity in his caricatures of ancient peoples as barbarians, we moved to a consideration of ancient teachings and an investigation of the correspondences between aspects of color and other processes of nature. As we would later work with numbers to provide ourselves with a technique to increase self-awareness, we correlated the underlying significance of numerical symbols to reality.

In the number 2 we noted the initial differentiation of life into its dual phases of positive force and negative form, of masculine and feminine principles. We saw absorption and reflection as comparable to the centripetal and centrifugal forces in physics. Through the constant pulsation of alternation in life we discussed the Wave Theory of light with its dual phases of crests and troughs. Noting duality in the contrast between the absolutes of white and black, light and no-light, we related the heavier, longer wavelengths of color to the physical end of the spectrum and the faster, more vibratory wavelengths to the spiritual end of the spectrum. From the spiritual teachings we understood man to have both an outer, physical aspect and an inner, spiritual aspect to his being. We became more aware of our own duality from the physiological systems in our bodies—in our metabolism with the dual functions of anabolism and catabolism, in our nervous system with the motor and sensory functions, in the division of our brain between the left and right hemispheres, in our respiratory system with its inhalation and exhalation.

Realizing the need to balance these two forces in nature, we progressed to the number 3, representative of the principle of reconciliation. In 3 we noted the dynamics of process, for from the minute atom through the activity of electronics we have in all vibrant life the process of 3 in operation. We related the dynamics of 3 to our vision of color, achieved as a result of the three systems of color reception in the retina of our eyes. Within our inner ear we observed the three semicircular canals by means of which we are able to maintain balance amidst the three coordinates of space. We saw the concept of 3 in the religions of Christianity with the Holy Trinity and Hinduism with the three Rishis. Through our awareness of the underlying significance of the number 3 we seeded our consciousness with the reality of relativity in all life. With this understanding of continual process in the stages of past-present-future, we could break away from an existence dominated by absolutes, dogmatism, and concepts fixed to a nonfunctional reality.

Proceeding to the number 7, we discussed the perfection of existence on this material plane to be represented by 7, linking as it does the 3 of the dynamics of life process with the 4 of the stability and foundation in material life. We noted this combination in man's body with the 3 indicative of the cranial, thoracic, and abdominal cavities, and the 4 suggestive of man's two arms and two legs. Citing the presently used five sense faculties of man, we intimated the development of two other sense faculties latent within man. From the occult teachings we learned of the seven rays of development and of the seven chakras of energy vortices located along the spinal column, through which man draws much of his energy from the universal environment. Aware that on our plane of existence cycles are often seven-phased processes, we referred to the seven-tiered spectrum of color and to the Law of Octaves. We observed this Law of Octaves in the Periodic Table, used in the classification of chemical elements. We recognized this law in operation, as well, in astrological science, where the three recently-discovered planets are considered higher octaves of similar energies symbolized by three of the seven "ancient" planets.

Cognizant of the significance of certain numbers to which we had referred in our scientific explanation of color, we advanced to the study of the primary colors. We saw red to be the most physical of the color energies. In orange we noted the blending of red and yellow, restraining the raw vitality of the physical with the initial seepings from the intellect. With yellow we came to the reasoning faculties given man as a species. From yellow we reached the mid-point of the color spectrum with green, representative of the balance and growth in nature. From the more physically oriented side of the spectrum we moved to the more spiritually oriented side. In blue we found a tranquillity, resulting from an innate faith in the life process. With indigo we observed the love and introspection of a philosophical attitude towards life. At the end of the color spectrum we arrived at violet, where inspiration gave stimulus to delve beyond surface appearance for the true reality of any situation. Because of our intention to synthesize color and number, we progressed beyond our seven-tiered spectrum of color. Using the Law of Octaves, we considered the first two colors of the next octave. We termed these two colors rose and gold, correspondent to the energies of red and orange respectively. In rose we saw the physical energy of red disciplined to turn visions into concrete realities. With gold we noted man's ultimate perfection, where there is a radiance from the state of consciousness.

As we had gained a basic understanding of the seven colors of the spectrum and the first two colors of the next octave of the color spectrum, the color-number technique was described. Recognizing all life as energy patterns, we learned that numbers, like colors, represent differentiated energies. Realizing that each individual is different with diverse functions to perform in this life experience, we sought in the science of numerology the symbols by which we could make ourselves more aware of who we are. For if we human beings, in accord with every life form in the universe, are energy patterns, then perhaps through mathematical formulas we can gain a greater understanding of our own individual structures. Similar to the spiritual teachings that each individual picks the conditions he or she intends to live through in this cycle of existence, we suggested that our names are mathematical structures to which our energy patterns resonate. But once we became aware of our numbers, we saw that we could not consciously work with the energies represented by the numerical symbols. Therefore, through correspondence we synthesized number and color. As a result, our color-number technique not only provides us with a means to increase self-awareness, but with this technique we have a daily tool in the form of color by which we can focus upon both the energies within our being and the energies deficient within us.

With the color-number technique we dissected our names into the components of our expression, our inner urge, and our latent self. We defined the expression as our calling card, the manner in which we present ourselves to other people. We explained the inner urge as the motivating factor, giving us the impetus to be the type of person we are. We described the latent self as representative of ourselves when we are alone relaxing without the need to strive. In our birthdate we found our destiny, the environment or external surroundings through which we are presented the opportunities to develop our lives. We saw how people can change the functions of their different characteristics by changing their names. After the mechanics of the color-number technique were detailed through the examples of two fictional guests, it was suggested that each of us construct our own color rainbow to discover what colors made up our expression, our inner urge, our latent self, our destiny, and the energies within us that were dominant and also lacking. For those doubtful of the rainbow's benefit we used our color-number technique to analyze briefly four well-known personalities: Jacqueline Lee Bouvier, Reginald Kenneth Dwight, Sophia Scicolone, and Jack Nicholson.

Informed as to the mechanics of construction and the mode of interpretation for our color rainbow, we decided to consciously apply color to our daily lives. To absorb into our bodies the energies of the colors of the spectrum we learned three color breathing and visualization techniques. With the Technique in Perceptive Awareness we sought to rebuild our concentration, which has been all but destroyed by the constant onslaught of external stimuli in our present-day society. Through the focusing of our attention on color and correspondent colored objects we acquired a method to become aware of both the multitude of mental distractions running through our minds and of our reactions to the various colors of the spectrum. Our second technique was the Conscious Imagination Technique where

181

we took control of our imagination to use it in a functional manner by imagining our ascent up a mountain of the color spectrum. At each plateau along our climb we paused to experience the level through the filter of one of the seven colors, starting at our base camp of red and culminating at the summit of violet. In the Technique in Energy Absorption we visualized ourselves as porous. As we breathed in, we filled every pore of our being with one of the seven colors. As we breathed out, we eliminated from our bodies the toxins from our patterns of living. After we had inhaled each of the seven colors, we ended with the absorption of white light.

With these three color breathing and visualization techniques to absorb internally the energies of color, we then learned how we could color the externals of our lives. Through decorating our homes, through dressing up our wardrobes, through coloring our daily meals with the intense fascination of an artist, we realized that we could improve the quality of our lives. Various hints of color use for the home were given in the form of colors to employ or avoid in the different rooms of the house, dependent upon the purpose of those areas. With our wardrobe we expressed the idea of accenting the colors of our individual color rainbows. We offered the effects of color in our apparel, noting in generalities how the different colors might present us and the reception we might get from other people. In our food selection we became aware that we are what we eat. By selecting foods based upon their color, we discovered a means to incorporate the different energies into our nourishment. We ended our last chapter asserting the possibility that through further investigation color's benefit to our health might eventually be proven to the satisfaction of our medical doctors. And now we approach the future.

What the future holds for each one of us is dependent upon what we do in the present. Although we are ending our journeys together, remember that every ending offers us a new beginning. We can begin to work upon ourselves. Each of us can start to improve daily our lives through this tool of color. Each of us has the responsibility to better our lives, for it can be done only if we do it. No one else can do it for us. We are the masters of our own destiny. We are the artists of our lives. And by increased awareness of ourselves and of the conditions that surround us, we can become master artists in the process of life. We have now gained one means to assist us in our purpose—the conscious use of color. As we work more consciously with color, we will see color become an ever more important part of our lives. We have seen color before. We will see color again. But its use can be infinite, as are the life energies color represents. Color can be incorporated in any environment. It can be used in any manner. By its conscious use we have a functional, working tool to improve our conditions and nurture our development.

As we end our travels together, let me wish you well. My thoughts go with you, for I am aware of how we can make this a paradise on earth through increased consciousness. We separate now in our journeys through life, for each of us has a different path to walk. Each of us has different experiences from which we might learn. But we can share with one another. For those of us who choose to share, for those of us who choose to develop ourselves, the time is now. No longer need our lives be frustrating and self-defeating, as if painted in blacks, browns, and grays. We can live like children in the constant awe and wonder of life's experiences.

This is the pot of gold at the end of the rainbow. And who could ask for more? By your becoming a master artist in the art of living, your life can become a garden of delights. From now on, you have the ability to color your world.

Bibliography

Abbott, Arthur G., *The Color of Life*, McGraw-Hill Book Co., New York, 1947.

Anderson, Mary, *Colour Healing*, Samuel Weiser Inc., New York, 1975.

Avery, Kevin Quinn, *The Numbers of Life*, Freeway Press, New York, 1974.

Babbitt, Edwin S., *The Principles of Light and Color*, University Books, New Hyde Park, New York, 1967.

Bailey, Alice A., *Esoteric Psychology*, Vol. I, Lucis Publishing Co., New York, 1936.

Basford, Leslie, and Pick, Joan, *The Rays of Light*, Sampson Low, Marston and Co., London, 1966.

Birren, Faber, *Color Psychology and Color Therapy*, University Books, Secaucus, N. J., 1961.

Birren, Faber, *History of Color in Painting*, Reinhold Publishing Corp., New York, 1965.

Birren, Faber, *New Horizons in Color*, Reinhold Publishing Corp., New York, 1955.

Bragg, Sir William, *The Universe of Light*, Dover Publications, Inc., New York, 1959.

Burgoyne, Thomas H., *The Light of Egypt*, Vol. I, Astro Philosophical Publishing Co., Denver, 1963.

Campbell, Florence, *Your Days Are Numbered*, The Gateway, Ferndale, Pa., 1975.

Cheasley, Clifford W., *Numerology*, Health Research, Mokelumne Hill, Calif., 1972.

Cheasley, Clifford W., *What's in Your Name?*, Health Research, Mokelumne Hill, Calif., 1968.

Chevreul, M.E., *The Principles of Harmony and Contrast of Colours*, Bell & Daldy, London, 1870.

Collin, Rodney, *The Theory of Celestial Influence*, Samuel Weiser Inc., New York, 1975.

Color, Time-Life Books, New York, 1970.

Color Healing, Health Research, Mokelumne Hill, Calif., 1965.

Curtiss, Harriette Augusta, and Curtiss, F. Homer, *The Message of Aquaria*, The Curtiss Philosophic Book Co., Washington, D.C., 1938.

Curtiss, Harriette Augusta & Curtiss, F. Homer, *The Voice of Isis*, The Curtiss Philosophic Book Co., Washington, D.C., 1926.

deBary, Wm. Theodore (General Editor), *Sources of Indian Tradition*, Vol. I, Columbia University Press, New York and London, 1958.

Eeman, L.E., *The Technique of Conscious Evolution*, The C.W. Daniel Co., Ltd., Ashingdon, England, 1956.

Evans, Ralph M., *An Introduction to Color*, John Wiley & Sons, Inc., New York, 1948.

Fabri, Ralph, *Color: A Complete Guide for Artists*, Watson-Guptill Publications, New York, 1967.

Goethe, Johann Wolfgang von, *Theory of Colours* (translated by Charles Lock Eastlake), The M.I.T. Press, Cambridge, Mass., 1970.

Graves, Maitland, *The Art of Color and Design*, McGraw-Hill Book Co., New York, 1941.

Graves, Maitland, *Color Fundamentals*, McGraw-Hill Book Co., New York, 1952.

Guptill, Arthur L., *Color in Sketching and Rendering*, Reinhold Publishing Corp., New York, 1935.

Guptill, Arthur L., *Color Manual for Artists*, Reinhold Publishing Corp., New York.

Hall, Manly P., *Man, The Grand Symbol of the Mysteries*, The Philosophical Research Society, Los Angeles, 1972.

Heline, Corinne, *Color and Music in the New Age*, New Age Press, Inc., La Canada, Calif., 1964.

Heline, Corinne, *Healing and Regeneration Through Color*, New Age Press, Inc., La Canada, Calif., 1975.

Hunt, Roland T., *The Eighth Key To Colour*, L.N. Fowler & Co., Ltd., London, 1965.

Hunt, Roland T., *Fragrant and Radiant Healing Symphony*, 1937.

Hunt, Roland T., *The Seven Keys to Colour Healing*, The C.W. Daniel Company Ltd., London, 1971.

Jacobson, Egbert, *Basic Color*, Paul Theobald, Chicago, 1948.

Jordan, Juno, *Numerology: The Romance in Your Name*, J.F. Rowny Press, Santa Barbara, Calif., 1965.

Kandinsky, Wassily, *The Art of Spiritual Harmony*, Houghton Mifflin Co., Boston, 1914.

Katz, David, *The World of Color*, Kegan Paul, Trench, Trubner & Co., London, 1935.

Kilner, Walter J., *The Aura*, Samuel Weiser, Inc., New York, 1973.

Klein, Adrian Bernard, *Colour-Music*, Lockwood & Son, London, 1930.

Ladd-Franklin, Christine, *Colour and Colour Theories*, Harcourt, Brace & Co., New York, 1929.

Lakhovsky, Georges, *The Secrets of Life* (translated by Mark Clement), True Health Publishing Co., Stockwell, England, 1951.

Lawrence, D.H., *The Complete Short Stories*, Vol. II, Viking Press, New York, 1961.

Luckiesh, Matthew, *Color and Colors*, D. Van Nostrand Co., Inc., New York, 1938.

Luckiesh, Matthew, *Color and Its Applications*, D. Van Nostrand Co., Inc., New York, 1921.

Lüscher, Max, *The Lüscher Color Test* (translated and edited by Ian Scott), Pocket Books, New York, 1971.

Maerz, A. & Paul, M.R., *A Dictionary of Color*, McGraw-Hill Book Co., New York, 1930.

Magus Incognito, *The Secret Doctrines of the Rosicrucians*, Occult Press, Chicago, 1949.

Mayer, Gladys, *Colour and Healing*, New Knowledge Books, Horsham, Sussex, England, 1960.

Munsell, Albert H., *A Color Notation*, Munsell Color Co., Baltimore, Maryland, 1936.

Ostwald, Wilhelm, *Colour Science*, Winsor & Newton Ltd., London, 1931.

Ouseley, S.G.J., *The Power of the Rays*, L.N. Fowler & Co. Ltd., London, 1951.

Raleigh, A.S., *Hermetic Science of Motion and Number*, George W. Wiggs, Chicago, 1924.

Raleigh, A.S., *Metaphysical Healing*, Vol. II, The Hermetic Publishing Company, London, 1932.

Ramadahn, *Colour and Healing for the New Age* (through the mediumship of Ursula Roberts), published by Ursula Roberts, London.

Reichenbach, Hans, *Atom and Cosmos* (translated by Edward S. Allen), The Macmillan Co., New York, 1933.

Renner, Paul, *Color: Order and Harmony* (translated by Alexander Nesbitt), Reinhold Publishing Corp., New York, 1964.

Sander, C.G., *Colour in Health and Disease*, The C.W. Daniel Co. Ltd., London, 1926.

Sargent, Walter, *The Enjoyment and Use of Color*, Charles Scribner's Sons, New York, 1923.

Schindler, Maria, *Goethe's Theory of Colour*, New Knowledge Books, Sussex, England, 1964.

Stevens, Ernest J., *Lights, Colors, Tones and Nature's Finer Forces*, Health Research, Mokelumne Hill, Calif., 1974.

Sturzaker, Doreen and James, *Colour and the Kabbalah*, Samuel Weiser Inc., New York, 1975.

Taylor, Ariel Yvon and Hyer, H. Warren, *Numerology—Its Facts and Secrets*, C. & R. Anthony, Inc., New York, 1956.

Valla, Mary, *The Power of Numbers*, DeVorss & Co., Santa Monica, Calif., 1971.

Weizsacker, C.F. von and Juilfs, J., *Contemporary Physics* (translated by Arnold J. Pomerans), George Braziller, New York, 1962.

Wright, W.D., *The Measurement of Colour*, Adam Hilger Ltd., London, 1944.

Wright, W.D., *The Rays Are Not Coloured*, Adam Hilger Ltd., London, 1967.